KNIGHTS TEMPLAR

TACTICS AND DRILL

WITH THE

WORKING TEXT AND BURIAL SERVICE

OF THE

ORDERS OF KNIGHTHOOD,

AS ADOPTED BY THE

GRAND COMMANDERY OF THE STATE OF MICHIGAN.

BY ELLERY IRVING GARFIELD,
E. G. C. G., GRAND COMMANDERY OF MICHIGAN.

DETROIT:
PUBLISHED BY E. B. SMITH & CO.
1871.

Bound by Wm. Suckert, Detroit.

Detroit Free Press Print.

GRAND COMMANDERY OF KNIGHTS TEMPLAR,
STATE OF MICHIGAN,
Jackson, Jan'y 25, A. D. 1871, A. O. 753.

To Eminent Sir Oliver Bourke, Grand Recorder of the Grand Commandery of the State of Michigan:

The new system of Tactics prepared by ELLERY IRVING GARFIELD, E. G. C. G., of the Grand Commandery, having been approved and adopted by that body, you will cause the same to be published for the instruction of all Subordinate Commanderies in this jurisdiction.

Courteously yours,

JOHN L. MITCHELL,
Grand Commander.

OFFICE OF THE GRAND RECORDER OF THE GRAND COMMANDERY OF THE STATE OF MICHIGAN,
Detroit, Jan'y 27, A. D. 1871, A. O., 753.

To Eminent Sir Ellery I. Garfield, E. Grand Captain General:

You are hereby authorized to publish, for the instruction of all Subordinate Commanderies in this jurisdiction, the Tactics and Drill approved and adopted at the last Annual Conclave of the Grand Commandery of the State of Michigan.

By order of the R. E. Grand Commander,

(SEAL)

OLIVER BOURKE,
Grand Recorder.

INTRODUCTORY.

AT the Annual Conclave of the Grand Commandery of this State, held at Detroit, in June, 1869, the subject of Tactics for Knights Templar was brought up and discussed, when it was found that no two Commanderies used the same system; in fact, each had a style peculiar to itself. To secure uniformity, a committee was appointed, consisting of Sir Charles H. Brown, P. E. C., of Peninsular Commandery, of Kalamazoo, and Sir S. S. Mathews, C. G., of Pontiac Commandery, with the author as chairman, to report a system for adoption throughout the State, and this work is the result.

The advantages claimed for this system are:

1. The brevity of the commands, at the same time expressing in full the movement to be executed.

2. The readiness with which the principles may be acquired.

3. That the handsome and intricate movements peculiar to our Order are in this work rendered much handsomer, and less difficult of execution.

That the report met the expectations of the Grand Commandery, is evidenced by the promptness with which it was approved and adopted, and by the ease and rapidity with which the Commanderies of this

State, with comparatively little instruction, have become proficient in the tactics.

The author takes this opportunity to express his obligations to his fellow members of the committee for many valuable hints and suggestions.

A supplementary work, for the instruction of Commanderies in battalion movements and for camp duty, is in manuscript, and will be published soon.

SUGGESTIONS

TO THE CAPTAIN-GENERAL OR INSTRUCTOR OF A COMMANDERY.

In many Commanderies the number of Sir Knights is so small that it will not admit of assigning each officer to his position. For instance, the Cross cannot be formed properly with less than thirty Sir Knights, exclusive of the officers, and there are many Commanderies that cannot turn out this number. It would seem to be best that, until the number should be sufficient, all except the three principal officers and Prelate should assist in filling up the ranks. If necessary, the Sword Bearer and Warder could march in the ranks; however, this is left to the good sense and judgment of the officers.

Unless the number of Sir Knights on parade exceed one hundred, it would be best to use the single rank formation.

For convenience at dress parade and review, the Sir Knight on the extreme right and left of the line will act as right and left guides. If, as at a dress parade of a single Commandery, the Commandery is divided so as to form two or more divisions, there should be a right and left guide for each division, and at the command, *Rear, open order*, the right guide of each division, and the left guide of the left division, will step four paces to the rear.

In the single rank formation for dress parade or review, a very good way of obviating the delay of forming in double ranks, is to *count twos*, which can be done in the Asylum (the standard and guard do not count), and at the command, *Rear, open order*, MARCH, all number one Sir Knights stand fast and cast the head and eyes to the right; all number two Sir Knights step to the rear and dress on the guides. The author is aware that this is entirely a new movement, but it avoids the necessity of lessening the front of the Commanderies, which is a great desideratum, as the majority of our Commanderies cannot turn out to exceed fifty swords. The above is not laid down as a rule, but is given as a suggestion, and appears much better in practice than upon paper.

Let it be distinctly understood that the guide in marching right in front is *left*: that is, in column of threes, number three is the guide, and two and one dress upon him; in sections or platoons, the Sir Knight on the left of the section or platoon is the guide. The guides should not only be careful to cover, but also to preserve the exact wheeling distance. Great care should be exercised in selecting Sir Knights as guides. The Sir Knights will dress invariably as above (unless marching left in front when the guide is right), as the left guide alone is held responsible for the steady marching of the sections or platoons. The Sir Knight on the right of each section or platoon repeats, in a tone only sufficiently loud for his own section or platoon to hear, all orders necessary for the different formations.

It will be noticed that in this work all double-quick movements are avoided. Gaining distance is accomplished by simply lengthening or shortening the step. This can be done in nearly all cases without losing the cadence of the step.

In the diagrams the officers are designated as follows:

1. Eminent Commander; 2. Generalissimo; 3. Captain-General; 4. Prelate; 5. Treasurer; 6. Recorder; 7. Senior Warden; 8. Junior Warden; 9. Standard Bearer; 10. Sword Bearer; 11. Warder; * Past Officers.

KNIGHTS TEMPLAR TACTICS AND DRILL.

Commands.

There are three kinds:

1. The command of *caution*, which is *attention*.

2. The *preparatory command*, which indicates the movement that is to be executed.

3. The command of *execution*, such as MARCH or HALT, or, in the manual of swords, the part which causes the execution.

4. The tone of command should be animated, distinct, and of a loudness proportioned to the number of men under instruction.

5. The command *attention* is pronounced in a clear, firm voice.

6. The command of *execution* will be pronounced in a tone firm and brief.

7. The commands of caution, and the preparatory commands, are herein distinguished by *italics;* those of execution by SMALL CAPITALS; the divisions are indicated by a dash (—). The parts of commands which are placed in a parenthesis are not to be pronounced.

Position of the Sir Knight.

8. Heels on the same line, and as near each other as the conformation of the man will permit;

The feet turned out equally, and forming with each other an angle of about sixty degrees;

The knees straight without stiffness;

The body erect on the hips, inclining a little forward;

The shoulders square, and falling equally;

The arms hanging naturally;

The elbows near the body;

The palm of the hand turned a little to the front, the little finger behind the seam of the pantaloons;

The head erect, and square to the front without constraint;

The eyes fixed straight to the front, and striking the ground about the distance of fifteen paces.

Facings.

9. Facings to the right or left will be executed as follows. At the command—

1. *Right* (or *left*). 2. FACE.

10. At the command *face,* raise the right foot slightly, turn on the left heel, raising the toe a little, and bring the right heel by the side of the left.

To Face to the Rear.

1. ABOUT. 2. FACE.

11. At the command *about,* each Sir Knight will turn on the left heel, bring the left toe to the front, carry the right foot to the rear, the hollow opposite to, and about three inches from the left heel, the feet at right angles to each other.

12. At the command *face,* turn on both heels, raise the toes slightly, face to the rear, bringing the right foot by the side of the left.

1. FORWARD. 2. MARCH.

13. At the first command, each Sir Knight will throw the weight of the body on the right leg, bending slightly the left knee.

14. At the second command, step off promptly with the left foot straight to the front, taking a step of twenty-eight inches.

HALT.

15. At this command, which should be given the instant either foot is coming to the ground, the foot in rear will be brought up by the side of the other.

1. *Mark Time.* 2. MARCH.

16. The Sir Knights, at the first command, will throw the weight of the body on the right leg, bending slightly the left knee.

17. At the command *march*, the Sir Knights will make a semblance of marching, by raising the feet alternately without advancing, and bringing the heels by the side of each other, observing the cadence of the step.

1. *Side Step to the Right.* 2. MARCH.

18. At the command *march*, each Sir Knight will carry the right foot ten inches to the right, knees straight, shoulders square to the front; the left foot will then be brought by the side of the right, then raising the right, and continuing the movement until the command halt.

19. Side step to the left will be executed in a similar manner.

To March Backward.

1. *Backward.* 2. MARCH.

20. At the second command, the Sir Knights will step to the rear with the left foot fourteen inches, reckoning from heel to heel, and so on with the feet in succession, till the command is given to halt.

1. *Right* (or *left*) *Oblique.* 2. MARCH.

21. At the second command, each Sir Knight will make a half face to the right (or left), and then march straight forward in the new direction. As the Sir Knights no longer touch elbows, they will glance along the shoulders of the nearest files toward the side to which they are obliquing, and will regulate their steps so that their shoulders shall always be behind that of the next Sir Knight on that side, and that his head shall conceal the heads of the other men in the rank. Each Sir Knight should preserve the same length of step.

To resume the Original Direction.

1. *Forward.* 2. MARCH.

22. At the second command each Sir Knight will make a half face to the right (or left), and march straight to the front.

Alignments.

1. *Right.* 2. DRESS.

23. At the command *dress,* the Sir Knights will turn the head and eyes to the right, shoulders square to the front, place himself on a line with the Sir Knight next on his right, and without opening his arms touch with his elbow that of the Sir Knight on his right.

24. The line being well aligned, the Captain General will command,

FRONT.

25. At this command, Sir Knights will cast their eyes to the front and remain firm.

26. Alignments to the left will be made on the same principles.

To Open Ranks.

27. The Commandery being in line, to cause the ranks to be opened the Captain-General will command—

1. *Rear Open Order.* 2. MARCH.

28. At the first command, the guides on the extreme right and left of the line will step off four paces to the rear, to mark the alignment of the rear rank.

29. The Captain-General will place himself, at the same time, on the right flank, and observe that the guides are on a line parallel with the front rank.

30. At the second command, the front rank of Sir Knights will cast their eyes to the right, the rear rank will step to the rear without counting the steps, halt slightly in the rear of the alignment, and dress to the right on the line established by the guides.

31. The Captain-General, seeing the rear rank well aligned, will command—

FRONT.

32. At this command, the guides will take their places in the front rank, and the Sir Knights will cast their eyes to the front.

To Close Ranks.

33. The Captain-General will command—

1. *Close Order.* 2. MARCH.

34. At the command *march*, the rear rank will close up as before.

35. If the Captain-General should desire to give the Sir Knights rest, he will command—

1. *In Place.* 2. REST.

36. At this command, they will no longer be required to preserve silence or steadiness of position, but they will always keep one heel or the other on the alignment.

37. If the command is—

REST,

38. The Sir Knights will not be required to remain strictly in their places.

To Dismiss the Commandery.

39. The command will be—

1. *Break Ranks.* 2. MARCH.

40. At the first command, the Sir Knights will bring the left hand in front of the body, palm up; right hand over the left, palm down.

41. At the second command, bring the hands together smartly, and disperse.

MANUAL OF THE SWORD.

Draw—SWORDS.

42. (*First motion.*) At the command *draw*, seize the scabbard with the left hand near the mouth, at the same time passing the right across the body, grasp the hilt of the sword, and draw it about two inches.

43. (*Second motion.*) At the command *swords*, draw the sword by extending the arm full length, turn the hand, and bring the hilt to

the breast, the blade at an angle of about thirty degrees (same as *present*).

44. (*Third motion.*) Bring the right hand to the side, elbow a little bent and well back, holding the extreme end of the hilt between the thumb and two fingers, the blade perpendicular, resting against the point of the shoulder, the edge to the front.

Present—SWORDS.

45. At the command *swords*, raise the right hand, the guard level with the top of the shoulder, the flat of the blade opposite the right eye, at an angle of about thirty degrees, the elbow resting on the body.

Support—Swords.

46. At the command *swords*, raise the left hand (by bending the elbow) to the height of the breast, at the same time raising the right hand, and drop the blade into the left, the flat to the front, the right hand resting on the hip, the left forearm against the body, the blade at an angle of forty-five degrees.

Carry—SWORD.

47. At the command *sword,* drop the left hand to the side; at the same time bring the right to the side, at a position of *carry.*

Rest—SWORD.

48. At the command *sword*, bring both hands in front of the body, the left over the right, the arms extended nearly full length, the blade a little below the right shoulder.

RETURN—SWORDS.

49. (*First motion.*) At the command *return*, bring the sword to a *present;* at the same time seize the scabbard with the left hand near its mouth.

50. (*Second motion.*) Drop the point of the sword, turn the head to the left, and insert the point, so that the right hand is as high as and directly in front of the left shoulder, the sword nearly perpendicular, the head to the front.

51. (*Third motion.*) At the command *sword*, sheathe the sword promptly, bringing the hands to the side.

Parade—Rest.

52. At the command *rest,* drop the point of the sword until it reaches the ground between the feet; clasp the left hand over the right, at the same time carry the right foot three inches to the rear, the left knee slightly bent.

Attention—Sir Knights.

53. At the command *Knights*, carry the left hand to the side, raise the sword to the position of *carry*, at the same time bring the right foot to the side of the left.

Reverse—SWORDS.

54. (*First motion.*) At the command *swords*, bring the sword to a *present.*

55. (*Second motion.*) Extend the arm, drop the point to the left, carrying the blade to the rear, the blade supported by the elbow, the hilt at the height of the shoulder, the hilt carried between the thumb and two fingers, the sword across the right side, at an angle of 45 degrees.

Carry—SWORDS.

56. (*First motion.*) At the command *swords*, extend the right arm, turn the wrist to the right, and bring the sword to a *present.*

57. (*Second motion.*) Bring the sword to the position of *carry.*

SECURE—SWORD.

58. (*First motion.*) At the command *secure*, extend the left arm full length, the hand inside the scabbard, palm out.

59. (*Second motion.*) At the command *sword*, bring the left hand up, so that the back of the hand will rest a little above the left groin, the hilt of the sword resting on the forearm, the point of the scabbard directly in front of the right knee.

Return—SWORD.

60. At the command *sword*, drop the scabbard to the side, the left hand in its natural position.

Form—AVENUE.

61. At the word *form*, bring the sword to *present*; at the word *avenue*, extend the right foot about eighteen inches, and at the same time extend the right arm to its full length, directly in front, at such an elevation as to bring the right hand about on a level with the top of the head, the back of the hand turned to the left, the edge of the sword to the front, and cross the sword with that of the Sir Knight opposite. The swords should cross each other at about six inches from the points. When

properly done, the planting of the right foot and the crossing of the swords will be simultaneous. Care should be taken to keep the right arm straight, the common fault being to sink the elbow, and thus contract the avenue.

SWORD CUTS.

62. There are seven different ways of directing the edge of the sword, and seven only. These are numbered from one to seven respectively, and are technically termed *cuts*. Of the seven, four are made in diagonal directions, two horizontally, and one perpendicularly. The direction of each of these is illustrated in the following diagram:

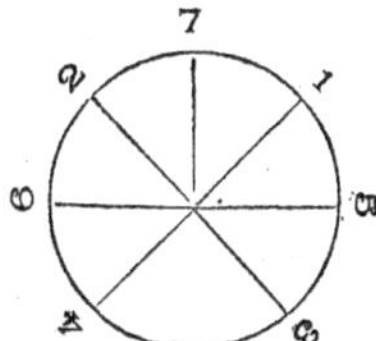

63. To make a cut with effect, and at the same time without exposing the person, two points require particular attention. The first is to acquire a facility in giving motion to the

arm by means of the wrist and shoulder, without bending the elbow; the second, to attain correctness in applying the edge in the exact direction of the blade. By a neglect of the first rule, the sword arm is exposed; and of the second, the blade will turn in the hand; and, as the flat part must receive the whole force of the blow, it will most likely be shivered to pieces. These rules, however, are of little force at the present time among Knights Templar, and the following instructions should be interpreted accordingly.

64. In all movements executed with the sword, the Sir Knight should bear the principal weight of the body upon his left leg, the right foot being advanced about eighteen inches to the front. The body should be well balanced, and the motions free from stiffness.

PREPARE TO GUARD.

65. At this command, the Sir Knight should stand square upon both feet, and bring his sword to the same position as *present,* the blade at an angle of about thirty degrees, or just sufficient to clear the chapeau.

GUARD.

66. At this command, advance the right foot about eighteen inches, resting the weight of the body principally upon the left, at the same time extend the right arm directly in front, the back of the hand nearly perpendicular to the rear, the flat of the blade to the front,* and cross swords with your opposite — the blades crossing each other about midway between the point and the hilt. This position should always follow *prepare to guard*, and always precede the

* In the real sword drill, the edge of the blade should be to the front, and the back of the hand upward.

cuts. The crossing should be simultaneous with the planting of the right feet.

Cut One.

67. To make this cut, turn the wrist so as to bring the point of the sword over the right shoulder, and then sweep diagonally down from right to left—or from one to four of the preceding diagram—bringing the sword back with a graceful motion to the position of *prepare to guard.*

Cut Two.

68. Bring the point of the sword over the left shoulder, and then sweep diagonally down from left to right—or from 2 to 3 of the diagram—bringing the sword back to *prepare to guard.*

Cut Three.

69. Turn the wrist so as to bring the point of the sword on the right near the ground, and sweep diagonally upward from right to left—or from 3 to 2—bringing the sword back to *prepare to guard.*

Cut Four.

70. Turn the wrist so as to bring the point of the sword near the ground, on the left, and

sweep diagonally upward from left to right—or from 4 to 1—bringing the sword back to *prepare to guard.*

Cut Five.

71. Turn the wrist so as to bring the point of the sword to the right, and sweep horizontally from right to left—or from 5 to 6—on a line with the neck, bringing the sword back to *prepare to guard.*

Cut Six.

72. Sweep horizontally from left to right—or from 6 to 5—on a line with the neck, bringing the sword back to *prepare to guard.*

Cut Seven.

73. Bring the point of the sword back over the head, and then cut down vertically—or from 7 to the centre—bringing the sword back to *prepare to guard,* as before.

74. These directions for giving the cuts are intended more particularly as a guide to individual practice, either with or without a diagram before the person exercising. Such practice is especially recommended for beginners, either in classes or singly, and should always precede exercising in couples. For

class practice, the Sir Knights should take distance by the point of the sword, the arm extended at full length. Although only a part of the above cuts are introduced into the *work* of Masonic Knighthood, and these much contracted, the occasional practice of all is recommended, as tending to secure a more free and graceful execution. In exercising by couples, the instructor should be careful to time his commands equally, thus: "*Prepare to guard—guard—cut two— one—four—two—advance—communicate—recover.*"

SALUTES WITH THE HAND.

75. (*First motion.*) Raise the right hand smartly as high as the mouth, pointing in the same direction as the right foot, the palm of the hand down, the thumb close to the forefinger, the arm extended.

76. (*Second motion.*) Bring the hand slowly around till the point of the thumb and the side of the forefinger touch the lower edge of the cap or visor, wrist and fingers slightly bent; at the same time turn the head a little to the left, and look toward the person to be saluted.

77. (*Third motion.*) Bring back the hand and arm to the position of the first motion.

78. (*Fourth motion.*) Drop the arm quickly by the side.

79. Left hand salutes will be similarly executed.

80. In saluting, Sir Knights will invariably use the hand farthest from the person to be saluted.

UNCOVER.

81. Raise the chapeau with the left hand from the head, and let it rest upon the right shoulder, the left forearm on the breast.

MANUAL FOR OFFICERS.

SALUTE WITH THE SWORD.

82. (*First motion.*) At the distance of six paces from the person to be saluted, raise the sword perpendicularly, the point up, the flat of the blade opposite to the right eye, the guard at the height of the shoulder, the elbow close to the body.

83. (*Second motion.*) Drop the point of the sword by extending the arm so that the right hand may be brought to the side of the right thigh, the back of the hand down, and remain

until the person to whom the salute is rendered shall be passed, or shall have passed six paces.

84. (*Third motion.*) Raise the sword to the position of *carry*.

85. In saluting with the sword, as at dress parade or review, the first motion will be executed at the command *present;* the second at the command *sword;* the third motion will be executed as the swords are brought to the *carry*.

86. When swords are returned at dress parade, the officers will drop the points of their swords to the ground, the back of the hand up.

COLOR SALUTE.

87. In the ranks, the Standard Bearer, whether at a halt or in march, will always carry the heel of the color staff supported at the right hip, the right hand generally placed on the staff at the height of the shoulder, to hold it steady. When the Standard has to render honors, the Standard Bearer will salute as follows:

88. At the distance of six paces from the person to be saluted, slip the right hand along the staff to the height of the eye; lower the

staff by straightening the arm to its full extent, the heel of the staff remaining at the hip. Bring back the staff to the habitual position, when the person saluted shall be passed, or shall have passed six paces.

TACTICS FOR THE ASYLUM.

TO FORM ESCORT,

89. The officer in charge will command—

1. *Fall in.* 2. FRONT. 3. RIGHT DRESS. 4. FRONT. 5. COUNT TWOS.

90. In this formation number one Sir Knights are the pivot men, number two wheeling up to the left of one.

91. The officer will then command—

1. *Twos Right.* 2. MARCH. 3. FORWARD.

92. The command *forward* will be given the instant the wheel of twos is completed to the right. At the proper place the officer will command—

1. *Open Order.* 2. MARCH.

93. At the second command the Sir Knights will oblique to the right and left, so that there will be an intèrval of about three paces between the divisions, and then march forward.

94. The officer will then command—

1. HALT. 2. *Inward* — FACE. 3. *Present*— SWORDS.

95. The Sir Knights will remain in this position until the * * * * * has passed through the lines, when the officer in charge of the escort will command—

1. *Carry* — SWORDS. 2. RETURN — SWORDS. 3. ABOUT—FACE. 4. *Posts.* 5. MARCH.

*RECEPTION OF S. M. OR E. C.

96. The Senior Warden will command—

1. *Attention, Sir Knights.* 2. FALL IN. 3. FRONT. 4. RIGHT DRESS. 5. FRONT.

97. This being completed, the Senior Warden will signify to the Captain-General that the line is formed, who will command—

OFFICERS—POSTS.

98. At this command, the officers will take their stations as follows: the Senior Warden on the right, the Junior Warden on the left of the line, the Standard Bearer, Sword Bearer

---

* The escort for the S. M. or E. C. is three Sir Knights; for the Grand Commander, six Sir Knights; for the Grand Master of the United States, nine Sir Knights.

and Warder at right angle to the left of the line of Sir Knights, facing the east, the Sword Bearer on the right, the Warder on the left of tho Standard Bearer.

99. The Captain-General will now direct the Senior Warden to repair, with the proper escort (three Sir Knights from the right of the lines) to the quarters of the E. C. (or S. M.) and inform him that the lines are formed and await his pleasure.

100. The Senior Warden will conduct them, by the rear of the line, to the quarters of the E. C. (or S. M.), and escort E. C. and G. through the lines. The Senior Warden and escort leads off—the E. C., G. and Prelate in order in the rear.

101. As the escort approach the left of the lines, the Captain-General will command—

1. *Present.* 2. SWORDS.

102. The escort return to their posts by obliquing to the right and halting in their former position.

103. The E. C. will now command—

Carry—SWORDS.

INSPECTION AND REVIEW.

104. The Sir Knights being formed in line, the Captain-General will take post three paces in front of the center of the line, and command—

1. *Prepare for Inspection and Review.* 2. *Rear Open Order.* 3. MARCH.

105. At the second command, the guides will step four paces to the rear.

106. At the third command, the ranks will be opened, and the Wardens and Standard Guard will step one pace to the front.

107. The lines being well aligned, the Captain-General will command—

FRONT.

108. The Captain-General will then face the east, and inform the E. C. that "the lines are formed for inspection and review," after which he will face the front, sword at a carry.

109. The E. C., with the Generalissimo, will then pass down in front of the Captain-General and first division, up in their rear, down in front of the second division, and up in their rear, to his position in the east. At the approach of

the E. C., the Captain-General will face about, and command—

Present—SWORDS.

110. He will then resume his former position and bring his sword to *salute*.

111. On the return of the E. C. and G. to the East, the Commander will command—

1. *Carry*—SWORDS. 2. *Close Order*. 3. MARCH.

112. At the second command, the officers will about face, and at the command MARCH will resume their former position in line.

REVIEW.

113. If the E. C. desires to have a review follow the inspection, he will direct the Captain-General to that effect.

114. The Sir Knights, being in line, will *count threes*, and the Captain-General will command—

1. *Threes Right*. 2. MARCH. 3. HALT.

115. He will then command—

1. *Pass in Review*. 2. *Column Forward*. 3. *Guide Right*. 4. MARCH.

116. The Sir Knights will march at a *carry*, the officers *saluting*, also the standard. The

C. G., having saluted, will place himself on the right of the E. C., and remain until the column has passed, when he will return to his position before the review. The head of the column having executed a second change to the left, after having passed the E. C., the Captain-General will command, *Guide left*, and, when it shall have arrived on the original line, HALT, form it in line to the left, open the ranks as before, and salute, which, being acknowledged, will terminate the review.

TO FORM THE SIR KNIGHTS IN TWO LINES, FACING INWARD.

117. In this movement all number one Sir Knights are in the first division, and are commanded by the Senior Warden; all number two Sir Knights are in the second division, and are commanded by the Junior Warden.

118. The Captain-General will command—

FORM LINES FOR REHEARSAL.

119. The Senior Warden will command—

1. *First Division*. 2. STAND FAST.

120. The Junior Warden will command—

1. *Second Division*. 2. *Forward*. 3. MARCH.

121. At the third command, all number two Sir Knights will march four paces to the front, when the Junior Warden will command—

1. HALT. 2. ABOUT—FACE.

122. And passes to the right of the second division, and then commands—

Left—DRESS.

123. At the last command, the Sir Knights of the second division will make one side step to the left, so that they will be exactly opposite the Sir Knights of the first division, and also align themselves, when the command will be—

FRONT.

124. When the Junior Warden will resume his post.

125. The above is also the manner of forming the lines for certain private rehearsals. It does away with the "Taking distance from the east by the point of sword."

126. To re-form in single line, the Captain-General will command—

1. *Second Division.* 2. *Forward into Line.* 3. MARCH.

127. The Sir Knights of the second division will oblique to the right and pass through the intervals of the first division, and one pace to the rear, when the Captain-General will command—

1. HALT. 2. ABOUT. 3. FACE. 4. *Into Line.* 5. MARCH.

TO FORM TRIANGLE.

128. To form triangle, the Sir Knights are first formed in single rank, and *count threes.*

129. The Captain-General will command—

1. *Threes Right.* 2. MARCH. 3. HALT. 4. *Close Order.* 5. MARCH.

130. At the fourth command, the first three will stand fast, and all the rear threes will close up at single rank distance, and at the command—

1. FRONT. 2. *Officers*—POSTS.

131. The officers will take positions as follows: Senior Warden on the right of the first division; Sword Bearer on the right of the second; Junior Warden on the right of the third; the Warder on the left, and the Standard Bearer in the center of second division.

132. In this formation all number one Sir Knights are in the first division; number two in the second; number three in the third; and will obey orders accordingly.

133. The Captain-General will command—

Form Triangle.

134. The Senior Warden will command—

1. *First Division.* 2. STAND FAST.

135. The Sword Bearer will command—

1. *Second Division.* 2. *Left—Face.* 3. *Forward by File Right.*

The Junior Warden will command—

1. *Third Division.* 2. *Forward.*

136. The Captain-General will now command—

MARCH.

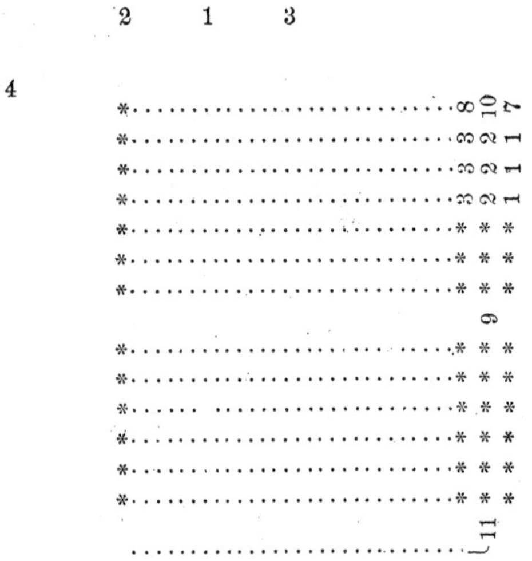

```
        2       1       3

4
        *..........................8 10 7
        *..........................3  2 1
        *..........................3  2 1
        *..........................3  2 1
        *..........................*  * *
        *..........................*  * *
        *..........................*  * *
                                      9
        *..........................*  * *
        *..........................*  * *
        *..........................*  * *
        *..........................*  * *
        *..........................*  * *
        *..........................*  * *
                                      11
         ..........................
```

137. When the third division will march forward a sufficient distance to allow the second division to form the base of the triangle, when the Junior Warden will command—

1. HALT. 2. ABOUT FACE.

138. Then pass by the rear to the left of his division, and dress them.

139. The second division will file to the right, and when the Sword Bearer has passed the left of the first division, he will command—

1. HALT. 2. FRONT. 3. RIGHT DRESS. 4. FRONT.

140. The Senior Warden will pass by the rear to the left of the first division.

```
*                         *
*                         *
*                         *
*                         *
*                         *
*                         *
*                         *
*                         *
*                         *
*                         *
*                         *
*                         *
8 11 * * * * * 9 * * * * * 10 7
```

141. The Captain-General will command—

1. *First and Third Division.* 2. *Left and Right Half Wheel.* 3. MARCH. 4. HALT.

142. The Senior and Junior Wardens will align their divisions, when the Captain-General will command—

RETURN—SWORDS.

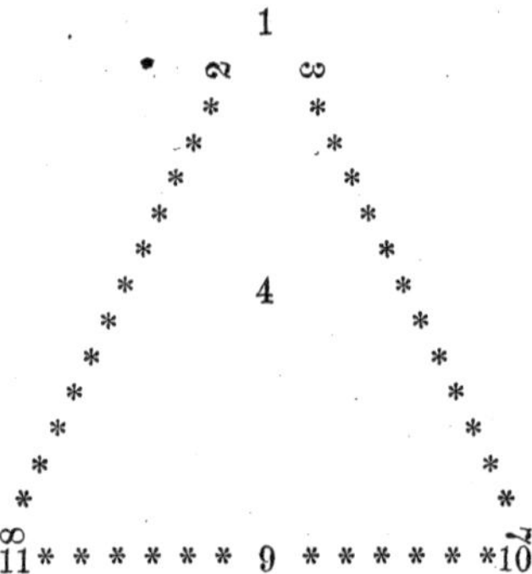

143. At the conclusion of the ceremonies for which the triangle was formed, the E. C. will command—

1. ABOUT FACE. 2. *Posts.* 3. MARCH.

TACTICS FOR PUBLIC PARADE.

144. The Captain-General will draw his sword and command—

1. ATTENTION SIR KNIGHTS. 2. FALL IN.

145. As soon as the Sir Knights are properly sized he will command—

1. FRONT. 2. RIGHT DRESS. 3. FRONT.

146. The Sir Knights being well aligned he will command—

1. COUNT THREES.

147. At the command *threes*, the rank will count off from right to left, *one*, *two*, *three*, each Sir Knight remembering his number.

TO MARCH BY THE FLANK.

148. The Captain-General will command—

1. *Threes right.* 2. MARCH. 3. *Forward.* 4. *Guide left.*

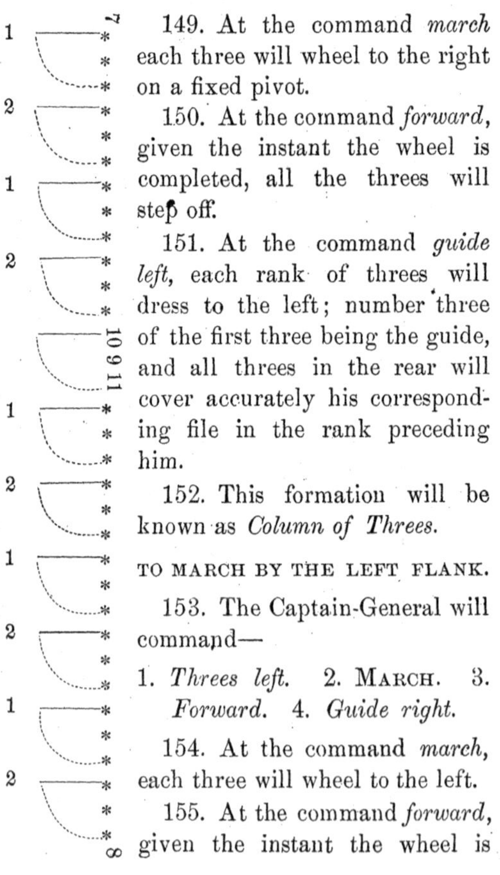

149. At the command *march* each three will wheel to the right on a fixed pivot.

150. At the command *forward*, given the instant the wheel is completed, all the threes will step off.

151. At the command *guide left*, each rank of threes will dress to the left; number three of the first three being the guide, and all threes in the rear will cover accurately his corresponding file in the rank preceding him.

152. This formation will be known as *Column of Threes*.

TO MARCH BY THE LEFT FLANK.

153. The Captain-General will command—

1. *Threes left*. 2. MARCH. 3. *Forward*. 4. *Guide right*.

154. At the command *march*, each three will wheel to the left.

155. At the command *forward*, given the instant the wheel is

complete, all the threes will step off, and dress to the right.

156. Should the Captain-General desire the Sir Knights to halt upon the completion of the wheel, he will command—

HALT,

157. At which the Sir Knights will halt.

CHANGE OF DIRECTION IN COLUMN OF THREES.

The Captain-General will command—

1. *Column right (or left).* 2. MARCH.

158. At the command *march,* the leading three will wheel to the right (or left) on a movable pivot, and then march straight to the front; all the other threes will wheel on the same ground.

To form Line from Column of Threes.

159. In column of threes, either at a halt or marching to form line to the right or left, the Captain-General will command—

1. *Threes right (or left).* 2. MARCH. 3. HALT. 4. RIGHT (OR LEFT) DRESS. 5. FRONT.

Form Line to March in Column of Threes to the Front.

1. *Right forward.* 2. *Threes right.* 3. MARCH. 4. *Guide left.*

160. At the command *march*, the right three will march straight to the front, shortening the first three or four steps, the other threes will wheel to the right. The second three will wheel to the left as soon as its first wheel is completed, and follow the first three. The remaining threes will follow to the left on the same ground.

161. The movement by the left will be similarly executed at the commands—

1. *Left forward.* 2. *Threes left.* 2. MARCH. 4. *Guide right.*

* *To March to the Rear.*

162. Being in line, or in column of threes at a halt or marching, at the command—

---

*Perhaps the best manner of instructing the Sir Knights in wheeling in column of threes is for the Captain-General to command—

1. *Threes in Circle Right Wheel.* 2. *March.*

At the command *march*, each three will wheel, as explained, for the fixed pivot. The threes will wheel around the circle several times, completing each arc of a half and full circle sim-

1. *Threes right about.* 2. MARCH. 3. *Forward.* 4. *Guide right.*

163. The command *forward* will be given at the instant the half circle is complete.

To March in Sections.

164. The first, third, fifth, etc., threes will be known as "odd threes." The second, fourth, etc., as "even threes." Being in column of threes, the C. G. will command—

1. *Form Sections.* 2. MARCH.

165. At the command *march*, all the odd threes will oblique to right, till they uncover the left or even threes; they will then shorten the step and march forward; when the even three arrive on a line with them, the guide will be left.

166. Great care should be taken in selecting guides for the different sections, as upon them

---

ultaneously. The precision of all movements by threes depends upon the immovability of the pivot, the touch of the elbow toward it, and the careful preservation of the distance of threes while marching. The instructor will therefore give these points his constant attention.

The above movement of *threes right about* can be used in columns of sections or platoons, or when marching at Commandery front.

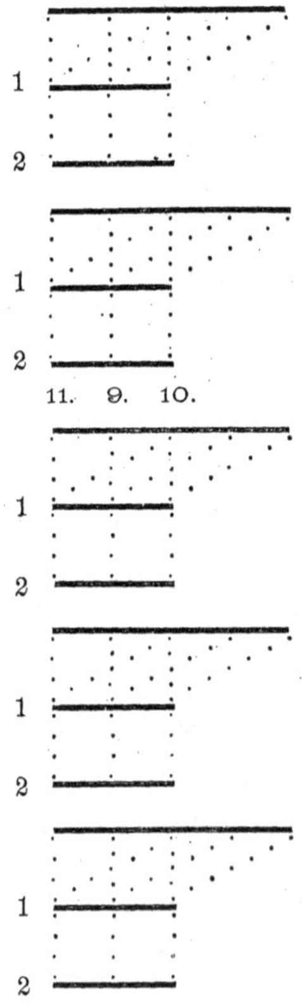
1
2
1
2
11. 9. 10.
1
2
1
2
1
2

depends the proper distances to be kept by the sections and the steadiness in marching. The Sir Knights on the right of each section should also be selected with care, as he has command of the section in many movements.

To form Column of Threes from Sections.

1. *Form Threes.* 2. MARCH.

167. At the command *march*, all the left, or even threes, will shorten the step until the right, or odd threes, are uncovered; the left threes then oblique to the right and resume their former position in column of threes.

To Form Platoons.

168. Being in sections, to form platoons, the Captain-General will command—

1. *Form Platoons.* 2. MARCH.

169. At the first command, the chiefs of the odd sections will command—

1. (*such*) *Section.* 2. *Right Oblique.*

170. The chiefs of even sections will caution the Sir Knights to march *straight forward.*

171. At the second command, *march*, all the odd sections will oblique to the right their own

front, which being done, the chiefs will command—

1. *Mark Time.* 2. MARCH.

172. The even sections having continued to march straight forward, when they shall be nearly up with the odd sections, the chief of the odd sections will command, FORWARD, and at the instant the two sections shall unite add, MARCH.

To Break into Sections from Platoons,

173. The Captain-General will command—

1. *Form Sections.* 2. MARCH.

174. At the first command, the chiefs of the odd sections will caution their sections to march straight forward.

175. The chiefs of the second sections will command, *mark time.*

176. At the second command, the odd sections continue to march straight forward; the even sections will *mark time.* The chiefs will immediately add—

1. *Right Oblique.* 2. MARCH.

177. The last command will be given so that when the obliquing is completed, and the com-

mand *forward, march,* is given, the sections may have their exact distance. The command FORWARD—MARCH will be given the instant the guide of the even sections shall cover the guide of the odd sections.

Wheeling from a Fixed Pivot, or in Marching.
1. *Section right wheel.* 2. *March.*

178. At the second command, the Sir Knights, except the pivot man, will step off with the left foot, turning at the same time the head a little to the left, the eyes fixed on the line of eyes of the Sir Knights to the left; the pivot man will merely mark time in his place, gradually turning his body, so as to conform to the movement of the marching flank; the Sir Knight on the marching flank will take the full step of twenty-eight inches, casting his eyes along the line, and feel the Sir Knight next him lightly.

179. The other Sir Knights will feel lightly the elbow of the Sir Knight next toward the pivot, resist pressure from the opposite side, and each conform himself to the marching flank, shortening the step according to the distance from the pivot.

180. In wheeling on a fixed pivot, the Sir Knights will constantly preserve the touch of the elbow toward the pivot; they will yield to pressure coming from this direction, while they resist that from the marching flank; they will cast their eyes toward the marching flank, and take steps according to their distance from the pivot.

Wheeling in Marching.

1. *First Section—Right Wheel.* 2. *March.*

181. The first command will be given when the section is three paces from the wheeling point.

182. At the second command, the wheel will be executed as on a fixed pivot, except that the touch of the elbow will be toward the marching flank (side of the guide) instead of the pivot; that the pivot man, instead of merely turning in his place, will conform himself to the movement of the marching flank, feel lightly the elbow of the next man, take steps of full nine inches, and thus gain ground forward in describing a small curve, so as to clear the wheeling point.

183. The wheel being completed, the Sir

Knight in command of the section will command—

1. *Forward.* 2. MARCH.

184. At the command *march*, given the instant the wheel is completed, the Sir Knight on the marching flank will direct himself straight to the front, and all the Knights in the section retake the full step of twenty-eight inches.

TO CHANGE DIRECTION BY THE SIDE OF THE GUIDE.

185. Being in column of sections or platoon on the march, with guide to the left, to change direction to the left the Captain-General will command—

Column Left.

186. The chief of the first section or platoon will command—

1. *First Section* (*or Platoons*). 2. *Left Turn.* 3. MARCH.

187. The first command will be given at three paces from the turning point.

188. At the second command, given the instant the change of direction should commence,

the left guide will face to the left and march straight forward without changing the cadence or length of the step. All the Sir Knights will lengthen the step, and place themselves on the right, taking the touch of elbow toward the guide upon arriving in line.

189. Right turn will be similarly executed.

190. The Captain-General may always effect a change of direction by a wheel, by first changing the guide to the side opposite the desired change, if not already there.

TO FORM COLUMN OF SECTIONS OR PLATOONS FROM LINE.

191. The Commandery being in line, the Captain-General will command—

1. *By Sections (or platoons)—Right Wheel.*
2. MARCH.

192. The sections (or platoons) wheel to the right, and when the wheel is completed the chief of the section (or platoon) will command—

HALT.

193. The sections (or platoons) are then dressed to the left.

TO FORM LINE FROM COLUMN OF SECTIONS AT A HALT.

194. The column having been halted, the Captain-General will command—

Left into Line Wheel.

195. At this command the right guides will caution the sections to *left wheel*, when the Captain-General will command—

MARCH.

196. The sections will then wheel to the left into line, the Standard Guard wheeling at the same time, and taking position to the front.

197. The Eminent Commander and Staff oblique to the left, and come in line according to rank.

198. The adjoining diagram illustrates the movement:

TO FORM COLUMN OF THREES FROM PLATOONS.

199. Being in column of platoons, right in front, to march to the front in column of threes the Captain-General will command—

1. *Right Forward.* 2. *Threes Right.* 3. MARCH. 4. *Guide Left.*

200. At the command *march*, the right three of each platoon will march straight to the front, shortening the first three or four steps; the other threes will wheel to the right. The second threes will wheel to the left as soon as its first wheel is completed, and follow the first three. The remaining threes will follow to the left on the same ground.

201. The movement will be similarly executed by the left at the command—

1. *Left Forward.* 2. *Threes Left.* 3. MARCH. 4. *Guide Right.*

FORM SINGLE RANK.

202. Being in column of threes, to march in single rank the Captain-General will command—

1. *Form Single Rank.* 2. MARCH.

203. At the second command, number one Sir Knights will march steadily forward; number two and three will shorten their step, and fall in the rear of number one.

FORM THREES FROM SINGLE RANK.

204. The Captain-General will command—

1. *Form Threes.* 2. MARCH.

205. At the command *march*, number two and three Sir Knights will oblique to the left, lengthen the step, and resume their position in column of threes.

206. The Commandery being in march in single rank, to form it in sections or platoons the Captain-General will command—

1. *By Sections (or Platoons) into Line.* 2. MARCH.

207. At the second command, the Sir Knight on the right of each section (or platoon) will march straight forward; the rear Sir Knights will advance the right shoulder, lengthen the step, and move into line by the shortest route, taking care to arrive on the line one after the other. As soon as the formation is complete, the Captain-General will command, *Guide left.*

208. Being in column of sections or platoons, to form single rank the Captain-General will command—

1. *Right* (*or Left*) *Flank.* 2. *By File Left* (*or Right*). 3. March.

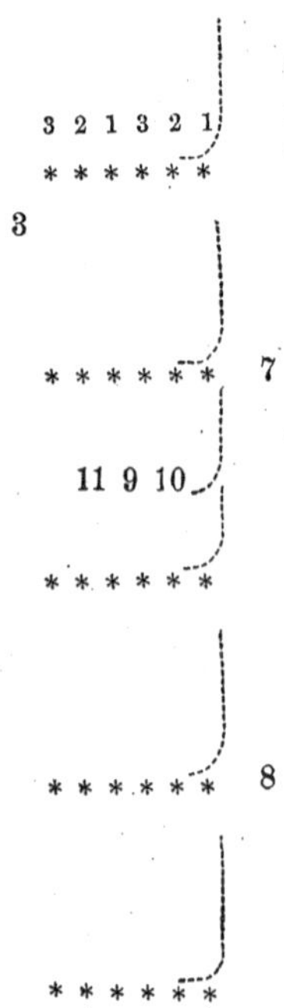

3 2 1 3 2 1
* * * * * *
3
* * * * * * 7
11 9 10
* * * * * *
* * * * * * 8
* * * * * *

209. At the command *march* each Sir Knight will face to the right (or left). The Sir Knight of the leading flank will immediately file to the left (or right); all the rear Sir Knights will file on the same ground.

ON RIGHT INTO LINE.

210. Being in column of sections or platoons right in front, the Captain-General wishing to form line on the right will command—

1. *On the Right into Line.* 2. *Guide Right.*

211. At the second command the Sir Knights will *guide right,* and continue to march straight forward.

212. The Captain-General having given the second command, will move to the point where the right of the line ought to rest, and place himself facing the point of direction to the left which he will choose.

213. The head of the column being nearly opposite the Captain-General, the chief of the section or platoon will command—

1. *(such) Section (or Platoon).* 2. *Right Turn.* 3. MARCH.

214. At the third command, the first section (or platoon) will *turn* to the right, in conformity to the principles prescribed for *right turn.* When the right guide shall be near the line, he will command—

1. *(such) Section (or Platoon).* 2. HALT.

215. At the command *halt,* which will be given the instant the right of the section (or platoon) shall arrive on the line, the section (or platoon) will halt, and the Sir Knights not yet in line will come up promptly and place themselves in line without the command, *right dress.*

216. The second section (or platoon) will continue to march straight forward, until its

right guide shall arrive opposite to the left file of the first; it will then turn to the right at the command of its chief, and march on the line, as prescribed for the first section or platoon.

217. In executing the right turn, and in marching on the line, the Sir Knights will arrive on the line one after the other, and immediately align themselves without command.

218. A column marching left in front will form on the left into line, according to the same principles, and by inverse means, at this command—

1. *On the Left into Line.* 2. *Guide Left.*

219. If marching in column of threes, the Captain-General will give the command of *march*, when each three will *turn* to the right at the proper place, number one being the guide.

FRONT INTO LINE.

220. Being in column of threes, in march, to form line to the front the Captain-General will command—

1. *Right* (*or Left*) *Front into Line.* 2. MARCH.
3. *Guide Left* (*or Right*).

221. At the command *march*, the first three will march straight to the front, shortening the step; the other threes will lengthen the step, oblique to the right (or left) till opposite their intervals, then march to the front, taking, upon arriving in line, the touch of elbow toward the guide. The guide will be announced immediately after the command *march*.

222. Being in column of threes, right in front, the Captain-General, desiring to form platoons, will command—

1. *By Platoons.* 2. *Left Front into Line.* 3. MARCH. 4. *Guide Left.*

223. At the third command, the right three of each platoon march straight forward, shortening the step; all the rear threes oblique to the left till opposite their intervals, lengthening the step, etc., as explained above.

TO FORM CROSS.

224. Being in column of sections, the Captain-General will command—

1. *Form Cross.* 2. MARCH.

225. At the first command, each Sir Knight in charge of sections will command as follows—

First Section. Right flank, file left.
Second Section. Right oblique.
Third Section. Forward. Guide right.
Fourth Section. Right flank, file left.
Fifth Section. Right flank, file left.

226. At the command *march*, each section will execute the movement indicated. The Sir Knight on the right of the first section shortens the step, for a few paces, to allow the rear sections to gain distance; the second section, as soon as it has obliqued its own front, will forward—march, and align itself on the Standard Guard; the Standard Guard having obliqued to the right, so that the Standard Bearer is directly in the rear of the left of the first section, the third section will gain distance and align itself also on the Standard, when the guide will be for the second and third sections, *center*. The fourth and fifth sections gain distance and march directly in rear of the Standard Bearer.

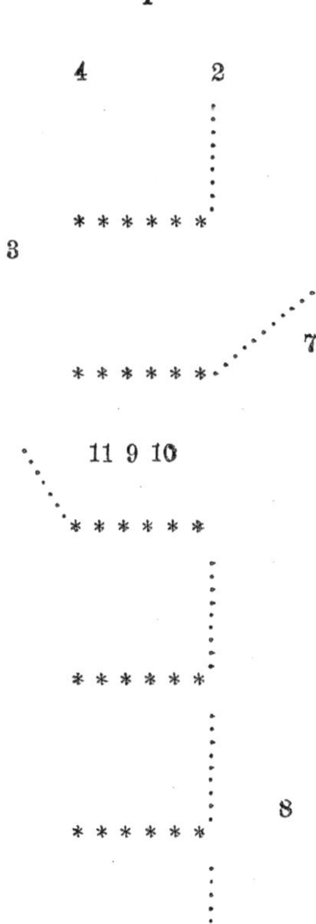
1
4
2
3
7
11 9 10
8

To Form Sections.

227. Marching in the form of a Cross, the Captain-General will command—

1. *Form Sections.* 2. MARCH.

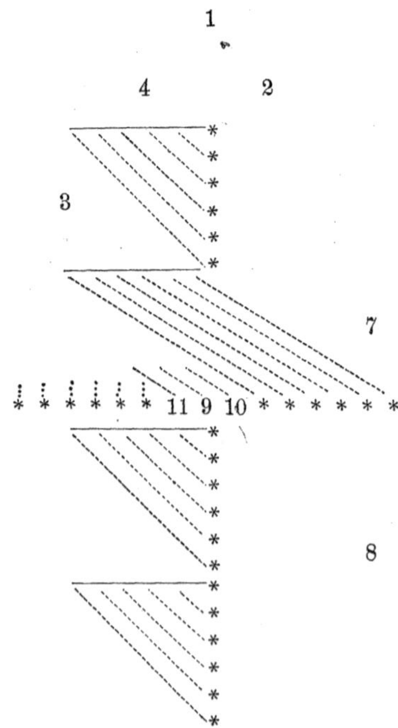

228. At the first command, the chiefs of sections will order as follows—

First Section. Into line.
Second Section. Left oblique.
Third Section. Mark time.
Fourth Section. Into line.
Fifth Section. Into line.

229. At the command *march*, the third section and Standard Guard will mark time until the second section is uncovered, and resume the forward when their proper section distance is gained. The fourth and fifth sections will also shorten step until the position is gained. As soon as the movement is complete the guide will be left.

To Form Double or Triple Cross.

230. Should there be more than five sections, a *double cross* can be formed with seven sections, and a *triple cross* with ten sections. In forming Double Cross, the commands for sections will be as follows—

First Section. Right flank, file left.
Second Section. Right oblique.
Third Section. Forward. Guide right.
Fourth Section. Right flank, file right.

Fifth Section. Right oblique.
Sixth Section. Forward. Guide right.
Seventh Section. Right flank, file left.

231. The fifth and sixth sections align themselves on the Sir Knight on the left of the fourth section.

To Form Triple Cross.

232. The first seven sections the same as above; the

Eighth Section. Right oblique.
Ninth Section. Forward. Guide right.
Tenth Section. Right flank, file left.

233. In this, the Standard should be between the fifth and sixth sections.

234. When there are ten sections, the first five sections may march in the Cross, and the rear five in the Triangle. If there should be more than ten sections, the above hints will answer for the different formations of a large body of Sir Knights.

BEING IN COLUMN OF THREES TO FORM TRIANGLE.

235. For this movement, the Sir Knights on the right of each division has command of that division.

236. The Captain-General will command—

1. *Form Triangle.* 2. MARCH.

237. At the first command, the Sir Knights in charge of each division will command—

1. *First Division.* 2. *Posts.*
1. *Second Division.* 2. *Mark Time.*
1. *Third Division.* 2. *Posts.*

238. At the command *march,* the chiefs of the first and third divisions will march steadily forward. Each number one Sir Knight will oblique to the right until his left shoulder is exactly in the rear of right shoulder of the Sir Knight in front of him, and march forward. In the same manner each number three Sir Knight will oblique to the left until his right shoulder is exactly in the rear of the left shoulder of the Sir Knight in front of him, and march forward, both divisions lengthening the step and closing up to half distance of threes. The chief of second division marks time, and all number two Sir Knights close up on him, at single rank distance, and then mark time. The Standard Bearer stepping out and marching forward until he has cleared the right of the second division, will, with the Sword Bearer

and Warder, march in the center of the triangle. As soon as the second division has closed up, the chief of that division will command—

1. *Into Line.* 2. MARCH.

239. And as soon as they shall have arrived in line, command—

1. *Right oblique.* 2. MARCH. 3. *Forward.* 4. MARCH. 5. *Guide right.*

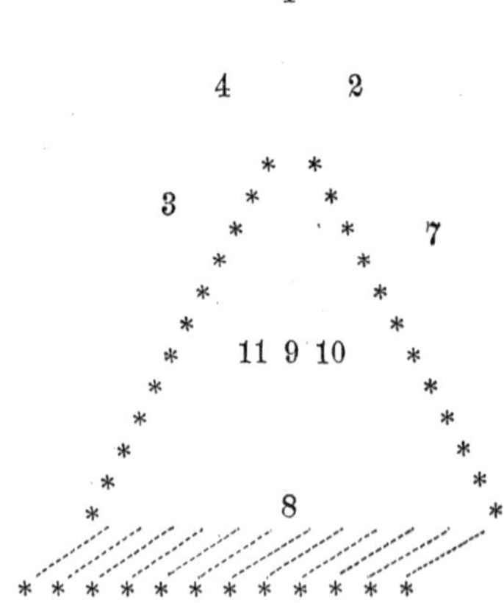

To Form Column of Threes from Triangle.

240. The Captain-General will command—

1. *Form Column.* 2. MARCH.

241. The chiefs of each division will command—

1. *First Division.* 2. *Posts.*
1. *Second Division.* 2. *Right flank, file left.*
1. *Third Division.* 2. *Posts.*

242. At the command *march*, the first and third divisions will oblique to their posts, those in the rear shortening their step to gain full distance of threes. The second division flank to the right and march to the left, and gain their position gradually by lengthening the step.

Double Rank Formation.

243. All the instructions given in this work have reference to the single rank formation.

244. When a Commandery numbers one hundred or more Sir Knights, the double rank formation can be used. The distance between the ranks should be sixteen inches.

245. If in two ranks, wishing to count off, the Captain-General will command—

1. *Each rank.* 2. COUNT THREES.

246. Having called off, either at a halt or marching, to march by the right flank, the Captain-General will command—

1. *Threes right.* 2. MARCH. 3. *Forward.* 4. *Guide left.*

247. At the command *march*, each three will wheel to the right on a fixed pivot, the rear rank Sir Knights simply covering their file leaders.

248. At the command *forward*, given the instant the wheel shall be completed, all the threes will step off, the front rank of each taking steps of twenty-eight inches, the rear rank shortening the step till they gain the distance of about twenty-four inches from the front rank.

249. At the command *guide left*, each rank will dress to the left.

250. Whenever the lines are formed, the rear rank will close up to the distance of sixteen inches.

251. All movements in the front rank formation are made by the same commands as in single rank, and the simple example given will answer for all movements.

252. In this formation the Senior and Junior Wardens will act as guides, whenever the ranks are opened, and at the command FRONT, step out to the line of officers.

DRESS PARADE OF A COMMANDERY.

253. The band or field music will take post on the right, the left of the front rank at ten paces from the right flank of the commandery.

254. All forms of ceremony may be executed in single rank by the same commands as in double ranks.

255. *The line being formed, commencing on the right, the Generalissimo and Captain-General will then successfully face about and command—

256. 1. (*Such*) *Division.* 2. PARADE REST; resume their front, and stand at Parade rest.

257. The left division having come to the parade rest, the adjutant will order the music

*When two more Commanderies are in line, the E. C. of each Commandery takes his position in front of the center of his Commandery, the Gen. and C. G. taking their positions at the command of *Rear, open order*—MARCH.

to *beat off*, when it will commence on the right, beat in front of the line to the left, and back to its place on the right, when it will cease. The adjutant will then step two paces to the front, face to the left, and command—

1. *Attention,* SIR KNIGHTS. 2. *Prepare to open ranks.* 3. *Rear, open order.* 4. MARCH.

258. At the words *Sir Knights,* the commandery will resume the *carry swords.*

259. At the third command, the guard on the right of each Division, and the left of the left division, will place himself four paces in the rear.

260. At the fourth command, the ranks will be opened, the adjutant aligning the rear rank; the Wardens, at the same time, will place themselves four paces in front.

261. The adjutant, seeing the ranks aligned, will command—

FRONT.

262. He will then pass along the front of the commandery to its center, turn to the right, and march to a point midway between the line of officers and the Eminent Commander, when he will halt, face about, and command—

Present—Swords.

263. At which swords will be presented, officers saluting. This done, the adjutant will face about, salute the Eminent Commander, and report: "*Sir, the parade is formed.*" The adjutant will then, on the intimation, "*Take your post, Sir,*" takes his post three paces to the left and one to the rear of the Eminent Commander, passing round his rear.

264. The Eminent Commander, while the band is playing, will stand at parade rest, with his arms folded, in which position he will continue until swords are about to be presented, when he will come to attention, and acknowledge the salute by touching his hat; the adjutant having taken his post, he will draw his sword, command: 1. *Carry*—Swords, and add such exercises in the manual of swords as he may desire, concluding with, *Return*—Swords. Officers will stand at the *carry* during the manual, and at the *return sword* they will drop the point to the ground.

265. He will then return his sword, and direct the adjutant to receive the reports.

266. The adjutant will now pass round the Eminent Commander to the right, advance

toward the line, halt midway between him and the line of officers, and command—

1. **Guards to the front and center.* 2. MARCH.

267. At the first command, the Guards will draw swords, step two paces to the front, and face inward. At the second command, they will march to the center and halt, when the adjutant will command—

1. FRONT. 2. REPORT.

268. At the second command, each in succession, beginning on the right, will salute by bringing the sword to a present, and will then report the result of the roll-call.

269. The reports being made, the adjutant will command—

1. *Guards outward*—FACE. 2. *To your posts*—MARCH.

270. At the command *march*, the guards will resume their places, and return swords. The adjutants will now face the Eminent Commander, salute and report.

271. The Eminent Commander will next

* The Guards are the right guides of each Division or Commandery, and do the duty of Sergeants.

direct the orders to be published, when the adjutant will face about, and command—

Attention to Orders.

272. He will then read the orders, after which he will face to the Eminent Commander, salute, and report. The Eminent Commander will then direct him to dismiss the parade, at which he will face to the line and command—

PARADE IS DISMISSED.

273. At this command, all the officers will return their swords, and face inward; they will then step off at the same time with, and close upon the adjutant, who will place himself in the line of officers; the officers having closed, the adjutant will command—

1. FRONT. 2. *Forward.* 3. MARCH.

274. At the third command, they will march to the front, dressing on the center, the band playing; arrived at six paces from the Eminent Commander, the adjutant will command:

HALT.

275. Upon which the officers will halt and salute, the adjutant and the officers to his right raising the right hand, those to the left, the

left. The hands will remain at the visor till the salute shall be acknowledged, and will drop at the same time with the hand of the Eminent Commander. The Eminent Commander will then give such instructions as he may deem necessary, which will conclude the ceremony.

276. As the officers disperse, the guards will close the ranks of their respective Divisions, and march them to the armory, where they will be dismissed, the band continuing to play until the commandery clear the parade ground.

REVIEW BY GRAND COMMANDER.

277. The Grand Commander will take his post in front of the center of the line.

278. The lines being in order, the G. C. G. will command—

1. *Prepare for Review.* 2. *Rear Open Order.* 3. MARCH.

279. At the third command the ranks will be opened, the G. C. G. aligning the Sir Knights in the front rank, the G. S. W. aligning the rear rank. The officers will advance four paces

to the front, as at parade; the standard bearer and guard will advance to the line of officers.

280. The G. C. G., seeing the ranks aligned, will command *Front*, and place himself, facing to the front, six paces in front of the line of officers, opposite the center of the line. The Grand Commander will now approach a few paces toward the G. C. G., and halt, when the G. C. G. will face about and command—

Present—SWORDS.

281. After which the Sir Knights will present, and officers salute; the standard will also salute. The G. C. G. will then face about and salute.

282. The Grand Commander will acknowledge the salute, and command—

Carry—SWORDS.

283. The Grand Commander will then proceed to the right of the line, and will pass in front of the officers to the left, returning to the right by the rear. While the Grand Commander is going round the line, the band will play, ceasing when he leaves the right to return to his station; the G. C. G., at the same time, will command—

1. *Close Order.* 2. MARCH.

284. At the first command, the officers and standard bearer will face about, and, at the second command, will return to their places.

285. The Grand Commander having taken his position, the G. C. G. will command—

1. *By Sections (or Platoons) Right Wheel.* 2. MARCH.* 3. *Pass in Review.* 4 *Column Forward.* 5. *Guide Right.* 6. MARCH.

286. At the second command, the Commanderies will break into column by sections (or platoons); the band will take position ten paces in front of the right of the line.

287. At the sixth command the column will step off, the band playing; the column will change direction at the points indicated, the G. C. G. taking his place five paces in front of the officers immediately after the second change. The band having passed the Grand Commander, will wheel to the left out of the column, and will take post in front of and facing the Grand Commander, continuing to play till the rear of the column shall have

* The sections or platoons will be halted by the C. G. of each Commandery on the completion of the wheel, and dressed.

passed, when it will cease, and then return to its original position before the review.

288. All officers will salute the Grand Commander when at six paces from him, recovering the sword when six paces past him. In saluting they will cast their eyes toward him. The standard bearer will also salute.

289. The G. C. G., having saluted, will place himself on the right of the Grand Commander, where he will remain until the left of the column shall have passed, when he will return to his position before the review. The head of the column having executed a second change of direction to the left, after having passed the Grand Commander, the G. C. G. will command—

Guide Left.

290. And when it shall arrive on the original ground, he will form it in line to the left, open the ranks as in the previous case, and salute; which being acknowledged, will terminate the review.

291. In passing in review the second time there is no saluting.

Reception and Escort to other Commanderies.

292. The Commandery to perform escort duty proceed to the place where they are to receive a visiting Commandery, and form in line faced to the front.

293. The visiting Commandery will then be notified that the escort is awaiting their pleasure, when they will march past the receiving Commandery, halt, and face to the front. The receiving Commandery will *present* swords while the visiting body is passing. The officers of the visiting Commandery salute, and the Sir Knights pass at a *carry*.

294. The receiving Commandery then break into column of threes or sections, and march past the visiting Commandery (the same manual being observed as before), who will fall in their rear as soon as their left has passed.

295. Arriving at the destination, the receiving Commandery will come to the front and *present*, the visitors marching past (officers saluting as before) into their quarters.

Position of Officers of a Commandery in Line.

8 * * * * * * * * * * * * * * * * * * 11 9 10 * * * * * * 3 2 1 3 2 1 7 3 * * 4 2 1

Position of Officers of a Commandery for Dress Parade.

1

3 2

8 * * * * * * * * * * * * * * * * * * 11 9 10 * * * * * * * * * * * * 7 Adj. 6 5 4

Position of Officers Marching in Column of Threes.

1
4 2
* 6 5
3 2 1
3 3 2 1
* * * 7
* * *
11 9 10
* * *
* * *
* * *
* * * 8
* * *

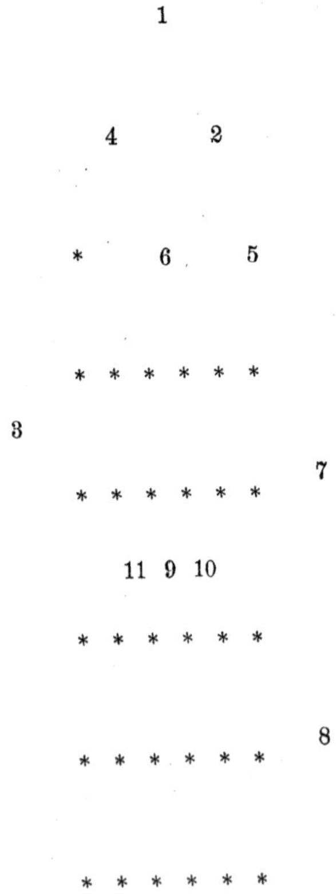

Position of Officers in Marching in Column of Sections.

1

4 2

* 6 5

* * * * * *

3

7

* * * * * *

11 9 10

* * * * * *

8

* * * * * *

* * * * * *

Position of Officers in Marching Single Cross.

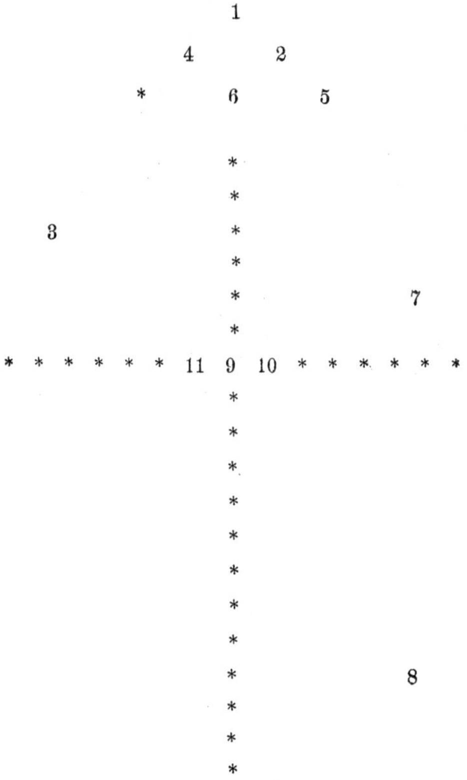

```
                     1
                 4       2
             *       6       5

                     *
                     *
     3               *
                     *
                     *                 7
                     *
* * * * * * 11  9  10 * * * * * *
                     *
                     *
                     *
                     *
                     *
                     *
                     *
                     *
                     *                 8
                     *
                     *
                     *
```

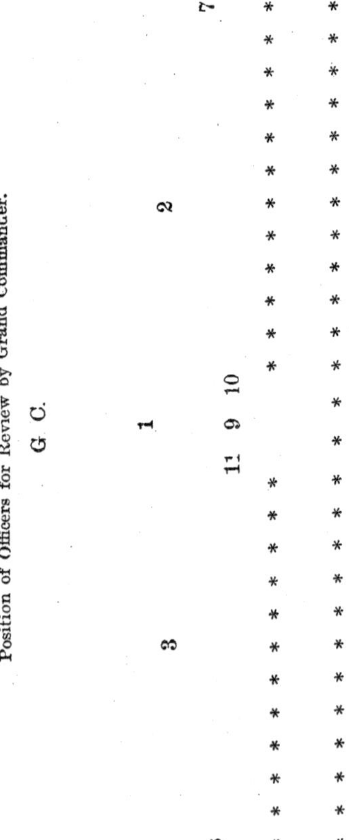

Position of Officers for Review by Grand Commander.

WORKING TEXT FOR THE ORDERS.

OFFICERS OF COUNCIL OF KNIGHTS OF THE RED CROSS.

Sovereign Master, representing King Darius, in the East; Chancellor, on the right, in the East; Master of the Palace, on the left, in the East; Prelate, on the right of the Chancellor; Master of Cavalry, on the right, in front of the Master of Finances, on the right of the first division when separately formed, and on the right of the whole when formed in line; Master of Infantry, on the left, in front of the Master of Dispatches, on the right of the second division when separately formed, and on the left of the whole when formed in line; Master of Finances, on the right, in front of the Chancellor; Master of Dispatches, on the left, in front of the Master of the Palace; Standard Bearer, in the West; Sword Bearer, on the right of the Standard Bearer; Warder, on the left of the Standard Bearer; three Guards at the several passes; and Sentinel, outside the door.

PRAYER AT OPENING A COUNCIL.

O Thou eternal, immortal, and invisible God; we would desire to come into Thy presence, at this time, with grateful hearts, to render thanks and praise for the wonderful display of Thy goodness and mercy. Be Thou pleased, O God, to be with Thy servants who are now assembled in Thy name; lift upon each one of us the light of Thy countenance; defend us from the evil intentions of our enemies, while traveling the journey of life; and when we shall finally come into Thy presence, to be freed from the chains of sin, and the sackcloth of repentance, be Thou merciful unto us, O God, not according to our deserts, but according to our necessities; and Thine shall be the praise, forever and ever. Amen.

Response.—So mote it be.

READING OF SCRIPTURE.

Now in the second year of their coming unto the house of God at Jerusalem, in the second month, began Zerubbabel, the son of Shealtiel, and Jeshua, the son of Jozadak, and the remnant of their brethren, the priests and Levites, and all they that were come out of the captivity unto Jerusalem; and appointed the Levites, from twenty years old and upwads, to set forward the work of the house of the Lord. Then stood Jeshua, with his sons and his brethren, Kadmiel, and his sons, the sons of Judah, together, to set forward the workmen in the house of God; the sons of Henedad, with their sons and brethren, the Levites. And when the builders laid the foundation of the temple of the Lord, they set the priests in their apparel with trumpets, and the Levites, the sons of Asaph, with cymbals, to praise the Lord, after the ordinance of David, King of Israel. And they sang together by course, in praising and giving thanks unto the Lord, because he is good, for his mercy endureth forever toward Israel. And all the people shouted with a great shout when they praised the Lord, because the foundation of the house of the Lord was laid.—*Ezra* iii.: 8–11.

Now when the adversaries of Judah and Benjamin

heard that the children of the captivity builded the temple unto the Lord God of Israel, then they came to Zerubbabel, and to the chief of the fathers, and said unto them, Let us build with you; for we seek your God as ye do; and we do sacrifice unto him, since the days of Esarhaddon, king of Assur, which brought us up hither. But Zerubbabel and Jeshua, and the rest of the chief of the fathers of Israel, said unto them, ye have nothing to do with us to build an house unto our God; but we ourselves together will build unto the Lord God of Israel, as king Cyrus, the king of Persia, hath commanded us. Then the people of the land weakened the hands of the people of Judah, and troubled them in building, and hired counsellors against them, to frustrate their purpose, all the days of Cyrus, king of Persia, even until the reign of Darius, king of Persia. And in the reign of Ahasuerus, in the beginning of his reign, wrote they unto him an accusation against the inhabitants of Judah and Jerusalem. And in the days of Artaxerxes wrote Bishlam, Mithredath, Tabeel, and the rest of their companions, unto Artaxerxes, king of Persia; and the writing of the letter was written in the Syrian tongue, and interpreted in the Syrian tongue: Rehum, the Chancellor, and Shimshai, the scribe, wrote a letter against Jerusalem to Artaxerxes, the king, in this sort: This is the copy of the letter that they sent unto him, even unto Artaxerxes, the king:—Thy servants, the men on this side of the river, and at such a time. Be it known unto the king, that the Jews, which came up from thee to us, are come into

Jerusalem, building the rebellious and the bad city, and have set up the walls thereof, and joined the foundations. Be it known now unto the king, that if this city be builded, and the walls set up again, then will they not pay toll, tribute and custom, and so thou shalt endamage the revenue of the kings. Now because we have maintained from the king's palace, and it was not meet for us to see the king's dishonor, therefore have we sent and certified the king; that search may be made in the book of the records of thy fathers: so that thou find in the book of the records, and know that this city is a rebellious city, and hurtful unto kings and provinces, and that they have moved sedition within the same of old time; for which cause was this city destroyed. We certify the king, that if this city be builded again, and the walls thereof set up, by this means thou shalt have no portion on this side of the river. Then sent the king an answer unto Rehum, the chancellor, and to Shimshai, the scribe, and to the rest of their companies that dwell in Samaria, and unto the rest beyond the river, Peace, and at such a time. The letter which ye sent us hath been plainly read before me. And I commanded, and search hath been made, and it is found that this city of old time hath made insurrection against kings, and that rebellion and sedition have been made therein. There have been mighty kings also over Jerusalem, which have ruled over all countries beyond the river; and toll, tribute and custom was paid unto them. Give ye now commandment to cause these men to cease, and that the city be not builded, until another commandment be given from me. Take heed now that ye fail not to do this: why should damage grow to the hurt of kings? Now, when the copy of king Artaxerxes' letter was read before Rehum, and Shimshai, the scribe, and their companions, they went up in haste to Jerusalem, unto the Jews, and made them to cease by force and power. Then ceased the work of the house of God, which is at Jerusalem. So it ceased unto the second year of the reign of Darius, king of Persia.—*Ezra* iv.

THE ROYAL BANQUET.

Darius, in the first year of his reign, gave a splendid and magnificent entertainment to the princes and nobility; and after they had retired, finding himself unable to sleep, he fell into discourse with his three favorite officers, to whom he proposed certain questions, telling them, at the same time, that he who should give him the most satisfactory answer should be clothed in purple, drink in a golden cup, wear a silken tiara, and a golden chain about his neck.

He then proposed this question:—Which is the greatest, the strength of *wine*, of the *king*, or of *women?*

On the following day the king assembled together the princes and nobility, to hear the question debated; and having placed himself upon the royal seat of judgment, he called upon them to make a public defense of their several opinions.

THE STRENGTH OF WINE.

O ye princes and rulers, how exceeding strong is wine! it causeth all men to err that drink it; it maketh the mind of the king and the beggar to be all one; of the bondman and freeman; of the poor man and of the rich; it turneth also every thought into jollity and mirth, so that a man remembereth neither sorrow nor debt; it changeth and elevateth the spirits, and enliveneth the heavy hearts of the miserable. It maketh a man forget his brethren, and draw his sword against his best friends O ye princes and rulers, is not wine the strongest, that forceth us to do these things?

THE POWER OF KINGS.

It is beyond dispute, O princes and rulers, that God has made man master of all things under the sun; to command them, to make use of them, and to apply them to his service as he pleases: but whereas men have only dominion over other sublunary creatures, kings have an authority even over men themselves, and a right of ruling them by will and pleasure. Now, he that is master of those who are masters of all things else, hath no earthly thing above him.

THE POWER OF WOMEN, AND OF TRUTH.

O princes and rulers, the force of wine is not to be denied, neither is that of kings, that unites so many men in one common bond of allegiance, but the super-eminency of *women* is yet above all this: for *kings* are but the gifts of women, and they are also the mothers of those that cultivate our *vineyards*. Women have the power to make us abandon our very country and relations, and many times to forget the best friends we have in the world, and forsaking all other comforts, to live and die with them. But when all is said, neither they, nor wine, nor kings, are comparable to the almighty force of *truth*. As for all other things, they are mortal and transient, but truth alone is unchangeable and everlasting; the benefits we receive from it are subject to no variations or vicissitudes of time and fortune. In her judgment is no unrighteousness, and she is the strength, wisdom, power and majesty of all ages. Blessed be the God of truth.

Response.—Great is truth, and mighty above all things. Ask what thou wilt, and I will give it thee, because thou art found wisest among thy companions.

THE KING'S VOW.

O king, remember thy vow, which thou hast vowed, to build Jerusalem in the day when thou shouldst come to thy kingdom, and to restore the holy vessels which were taken away out of Jerusalem. Thou hast also vowed to build up the temple, which was burned when Judah was made desolate by the Chaldees. And now, O king, this is that I desire of thee, that thou make good the vow, the performance whereof with thine own mouth thou hast vowed to the King of Heaven.

OFFICERS OF A COMMANDERY OF KNIGHTS TEMPLAR.

Eminent Commander, in the East; Generalissimo, on the right, in the East; Captain-General, on the left, in the East; Prelate, on the right of the Generalissimo; Senior Warden, on the right, in front of the

Treasurer, on the right of the first division when separately formed, and on the right of the whole when formed in line; Junior Warden, on the left, in front of the Recorder, on the right of the second division when separately formed, and on the left of the whole when formed in line; Treasurer, on the right, in front of the Generalissimo; Recorder, on the left, in front of the Captain-General; Standard Bearer, Sword Bearer, Warder, Three Guards, and Sentinel, the same as in a Council of Knights of the Red Cross.

PRAYER AT OPENING A COMMANDERY.

Our Father who art in heaven, hallowed be Thy Name. Thy kingdom come. Thy will be done on earth, as it is in heaven. Give us this day our daily bread. And forgive us our trespasses, as we forgive those who trespass against us. And lead us not into temptation; but deliver us from evil. For Thine is the kingdom, and the power, and the glory forever and ever. Amen.

EXHORTATION AT OPENING.

My brethren, count it all joy when ye fall into divers temptations; knowing this, that the trying of your faith worketh patience. But let patience have her perfect work, that ye may be perfect and entire, wanting nothing. If any of you lack wisdom, let him ask of God, that giveth to all men liberally, and upbraideth not, and it shall be given him. But let him ask in faith, nothing wavering, for he that wavereth is like a wave of the sea, driven with the wind, and tossed. For let not that man think that he shall receive anything of the Lord. A double-minded man is unstable in all his ways. Let not the brother of low degree rejoice in that he is exalted. If any man among you seem to be religious, and bridleth not his tongue, but deceiveth his own heart, that man's religion is vain. Pure religion and undefiled, before God and the Father, is this: To visit the fatherless and the widows in their affliction, and to keep himself unspotted from the world.—*James* i.: 2–10, 26, 27.

1. *Exhortation.*

.... I greet thee.

Silver and gold have I none; but such as I have give I unto thee.

—— —— —— —— —— ——

Hearken to a lesson to cheer thee on thy way, and assure thee of success.

And Abraham rose up early in the morning, and took *bread* and a *bottle* of *water* and gave it unto Hagar (putting it on her shoulder) and the child, and sent her away, and she departed and wandered in the wilderness, and the water was spent in the bottle, and she cast the child under one of the shrubs; and the angel of God called to Hagar out of Heaven, saying, Arise, lift up the lad and hold him in thine hand, for I will make him a great nation; and God opened her eyes, and she saw a well of water. By faith Abraham sojourned in the land of promise as in a strange country, dwelling in tabernacles; for he looked for a city which had foundations, whose builder and maker is God. Be ye therefore followers of God, as dear children, rejoicing in the Lord always; and again I say, rejoice.

Farewell..............God speed thee on thy way.

2. *Exhortation.*

..............I greet thee. —— —— ——

If a brother or sister be naked and destitute of daily food, and one of you say, Depart in peace, be ye warmed and filled, and ye give them not of those things which are needful for the body, what doth it profit? To do good and communicate, forget not, for with such sacrifices God is well pleased. Beware, lest any man spoil you through philosophy and vain deceit, after the traditions of men; after the rudiments of the world, and not after Christ: for in him dwelleth all the fullness of the godhead bodily.

Farewell..............God speed thee on thy way.

3. *Exhortation.*

..............I greet thee. —— —— ——

He that receiveth you receiveth me, and he that receiveth me receiveth him that sent me. Come unto me all ye that labor and are heavy laden, and I will give you rest. Take my yoke upon you and learn of me, for I am meek and lowly in heart, and ye shall find rest unto your souls, for my yoke is easy and my burden is light. Whosoever shall give to drink unto one of these little ones a cup of cold water only, in the name of a disciple, verily I say unto you he shall in no wise lose his reward.

Farewell..............God speed thee on thy way.

THE APOSTACY OF JUDAS ISCARIOT.

Then one of the twelve called Judas Iscariot, went unto the chief priests, and said unto them, What will ye give me, and I will deliver him unto you? And they covenanted with him for thirty pieces of silver. And from that time he sought opportunity to betray him. Now the first day of the feast of unleavened bread, the disciples came unto Jesus, saying unto him, where wilt thou that we prepare for thee to eat the passover? And he said, Go into the city to such a man, and say unto him, The master saith, My time is at hand; I will keep the passover at thy house with my disciples. And the disciples did as Jesus had appointed them, and they made ready the passover. Now when the even was come, he sat down with the twelve. And as they did eat, he said, Verily I say unto you, that one of you shall betray me. And they were exceeding sorrowful, and began every one of them to say unto him, Lord, is it I? And he answered and said, He that dippeth his hand with me in the dish, the same shall betray me. The Son of man goeth, as it is written of him: but wo unto that man by whom the Son of man is betrayed! It had been good for that man if he had not been born. Then Judas, which betrayed him, answered and said, Master, is it I? He said unto him, Thou hast said.—*Matt.* xxvi. 14-25, 36-49.

THE BITTER CUP.

Then cometh Jesus with them unto a place called Gethsemane, and saith unto the disciples, Sit ye here, while I go and pray yonder. And he took with him Peter and the two sons of Zebedee, and began to be sorrowful and very heavy. Then saith he unto them, My soul is exceeding sorrowful, even unto death: tarry ye here, and watch with me. And he went a little further, and fell on his face, and prayed, saying, O my Father, if it be possible, let this cup pass from me; nevertheless, not as I will, but as thou wilt. And he cometh unto the disciples, and findeth them asleep, and saith unto Peter, What! could ye not watch with me one hour? Watch and pray that ye enter not into temptation: the spirit indeed is willing, but the flesh is weak. He went away again the second time, and prayed, saying, O my Father, if this cup may not pass away from me, except I drink it, thy will be done. And he came and found them asleep again; for their eyes were heavy. And he left them, and went away again, and prayed the third time, saying the same words. Then cometh he to his disciples, and saith unto them, Sleep on now, and take your rest: behold, the hour is at hand, and the Son of man is betrayed into the hands of sinners. Rise, let us be going: behold he is at hand that doth betray me. And while he yet spake, lo, Judas, one of the twelve, came, and with him a great multitude, with swords and staves, from the chief priests and elders of the people. Now he that betrayed him gave them a sign, saying, Whomsoever I shall kiss, that same is he: hold him fast. And forthwith he came to Jesus, and said, Hail, master; and kissed him.

THE CRUCIFIXION.

When Pilate saw that he could prevail nothing, but rather a tumult was made, he took water, and washed his hands before the multitude, saying, I am innocent of the blood of this just person; see ye to it. Then answered all the people and said, His blood be on us, and on our children. Then released he Barabbas unto them: and when he had scourged Jesus, he delivered him to be crucified. Then the soldiers of the governor took Jesus into the common hall, and gathered unto him the whole band of soldiers. And they stripped him, and put on him a scarlet robe. And when they had platted a crown of thorns, they put it upon his head, and a reed in his right hand: and they bowed the knee before him, and mocked him, saying, Hail king of the Jews! And they spit upon him, and took the reed and smote him on the head. And after that they had mocked him, they took the robe off from him and put his own raiment on him, and led him away to crucify him. And as they came out, they found a man of Cyrene, Simon by name: him they compelled to bear his cross. And when they were come unto a place called Golgotha, that is to say, A place of a skull, they gave him vinegar to drink, mingled with gall: and when he had tasted thereof he would not drink. And they crucified him, and parted his garments, casting lots. And sitting down, they watched him there; and set up over his head his accusation written, *This is Jesus the King of the Jews.—Matt.* xxvii. 24–38.

THE RESURRECTION AND ASCENSION.

Although it is appointed unto all men once to die, yet, as the Scriptures inform, the Saviour of the world arose from the dead and ascended up into heaven, there forever seated on the throne of majesty on high, so they also assure us, that all who have received Him for their righteousness and put their trust in Him, shall rise to life everlasting. "In the end of the Sabbath, as it began to dawn toward the first day of the week, came Mary Magdalene, and the other Mary, to see the sepulchre. And behold, there was a great earthquake: for the angel of the Lord descended from heaven, and came and rolled back the stone from the door and sat upon it. His countenance was like lightning, and his raiment white as snow: And for fear of him the keepers did shake and become as dead men And the angel answered and said unto the women, Fear not ye: for I know that ye seek Jesus which is crucified. He is not here, for he has risen as he said. Come see the place where the Lord lay: and go quickly and tell his disciples that he is risen from the dead; and behold, he goeth before you into Galilee: there shall ye see him: lo, I have told you. And they departed quickly from the sepulchre with fear and great joy, and did run to bring his disciples word. And as they went to tell his disciples, behold Jesus met them, saying, All hail. And they came and held him by the feet and worshipped him. And he led them out as far as Bethany; and he lifted up his hands and blessed them. And it came to pass while he blessed them, he was parted from them and carried up into heaven. And they worshipped him, and returned to Jerusalem with great joy."

THE ELECTION OF MATTHIAS.

And in those days Peter stood up in the midst of the disciples, and said (the number of the names together were about one hundred and twenty), Men and brethren, this Scripture must needs have been fulfilled, which the Holy Ghost, by the mouth of David, spake before, concerning Judas, which was guide to them that took Jesus. For he was numbered with us, and had obtained a part of this ministry. Now this man purchased a field with the reward of his iniquity; and, falling headlong, he burst asunder in the midst, and all his bowels gushed out. And it was known unto all the dwellers at Jerusalem: insomuch as that field is called, in their proper tongue, Aceldama, that is to say, the field of blood. For it is written in the Book of Psalms, Let his habitation be desolate, and no man dwell therein; and his bishopric let another take. Wherefore, of these men which have companied with us all the time that the Lord Jesus went in and out among us, beginning from the baptism of John, unto that same day that he was taken up from us, must one be ordained to be a witness with us of his resurrection. And they appointed two, Joseph, called Barsabas, who was surnamed

Justus, and Matthias. And they prayed and said, Thou, Lord, which knowest the hearts of all men, shew whether of these two thou hast chosen, that he may take part of this ministry and apostleship, from which Judas by transgression fell, that he might go to his own place. And they gave forth their lots: and the lot fell upon Matthias; and he was numbered with the eleven apostles.—*Acts* i: 15–26.

EXHORTATION AT CLOSING.

Finally, my brethren, be strong in the Lord, and in the power of his might. Put on the *whole armor* of God, that ye may be able to stand against the wiles of the devil. For we wrestle not against flesh and blood, but against principalities and powers; against the rulers of the darkness of the world; against spiritual darkness in high places. Wherefore tak unto you the whole armor of God, that ye may able to withstand in the evil day, and having done all, to stand. Stand, therefore, with your *loins girt* about with truth. And having on the *breastplate* of righteousness. And *your feet shod* with the preparation of the gospel of peace. Above all, taking the *shield* of faith, wherewith you shall be able to quench the fiery darts of the wicked. And take the *helmet* of salvation. And the *sword* of the Spirit, which is the word of God.—*Eph.* vi: 10–17.

OFFICERS OF A COUNCIL OF KNIGHTS OF MALTA.

Eminent Commander, Generalissimo, Captain-General, Prelate, Senior Warden, Junior Warden, Treasurer, Recorder, First Guard, Second Guard, Standard Bearer, Sword Bearer, Warder, and Sentinel.

THE SHIPWRECK OF ST. PAUL.

And when they were escaped, then they knew that the island was called Melita. And the barbarous people showed us no little kindness: for they kindled a fire and received us every one; because of the present rain, and because of the cold. And when Paul had gathered a bundle of sticks, and laid them on the fire, there came a viper out of the heat and fastened on his hand. And when the barbarians saw the venomous beast hang on his hand, they said among themselves, No doubt this man is a murderer, whom, though he hath escaped the sea, yet vengeance suffereth not to live. And he shook off the beast into the fire, and felt no harm. Howbeit, they looked when he should have swollen, or fallen down dead suddenly; but after they had looked a great while, and saw no harm come to him, they changed their minds, and said that he was a god.—*Acts* xxviii: 1–6.

And Pilate wrote a title, and put it on the cross. And the writing was, *Jesus of Nazareth the King of the Jews.*—*John* xix: 19.

THE UNBELIEF OF THOMAS.

But Thomas, one of the twelve, called Didymus, was not with them when Jesus came. The other disciples, therefore, said unto him, We have seen the Lord. But he said unto them, Except I shall see in his hands the print of the nails, and put my finger into the print of the nails, and thrust my hand into his side, I will not believe. And after eight days, again his disciples were within, and Thomas with them. Then came Jesus, the doors being shut, and stood in the midst, and said, Peace be with you. Then said he to Thomas, Reach hither thy finger, and behold my hands: and reach hither thy hand, and thrust it into my side; and be not faithless, but believing. And Thomas answered and said unto him, My Lord and my God.—*John* xx: 24–28.

CHARGE TO A NEWLY-CREATED SIR KNIGHT.

Sir Knight: Having passed through the several degrees of our ancient and honorable institution, we bid you a hearty welcome to all our rights and privileges, even to that disinterested friendship and unbounded hospitality which ever has, and we hope and trust ever will continue to adorn, distinguish, and characterize this noble Order.

It will henceforth become your duty to assist, protect, and defend the weary, wayworn traveler who finds the height of fortune inaccessible, and thorny paths of life broken, adverse, and forlorn,—to succor, defend, and protect the *innocent*, the *distressed*, and the *helpless*, ever standing forth as a champion to espouse the cause of the *Christian Religion.*

You are to inculcate, enforce, and practice *virtue;* and amid all the temptations which surround you, never to be drawn aside from the path of duty, or forgetful of those due regards and passwords, which are necessary to be had in perpetual remembrance; and while one hand is wielding the sword for the defense of your companion in danger, let the other grasp the mystic Trowel, and widely diffuse the genuine cement of Brotherly Love and Friendship.

Should calumny assail the character of a Brother Sir Knight, recollect that you are to step forth and vindicate his good name, and assist him on all lawful occasions. Should assailants ever attempt your honor, interest, or happiness, remember, also, that you have the counsel and support of your brethren, whose mystic swords, combining the virtues of Faith, Hope, and Charity, with *Justice*, *Fortitude*, and *Mercy*, will leap from their scabbards in defense of your just rights, and insure you a glorious triumph over all your enemies.

On this occasion permit me, Sir Knight, to remind you of our mutual engagements, our reciprocal ties; for whatever may be your situation or rank in life, you may find those in similar stations, who have dignified themselves and been useful to mankind. You are, therefore, called upon to discharge all your duties with fidelity and patience, whether in the *Field*, in the *Senate*, on the *Bench*, at the *Bar*, or at the *Holy Altar*. Whether you are placed upon the highest pinnacle of worldly grandeur, or glide into the humble vale of obscurity, unnoticed, save by a few, it matters not; for a few rolling suns will close the scene, when naught but holiness will serve as a sure passport to gain admission into that REST prepared for the foundation of the world.

If you see a brother bending under the cross of adversity and disappointment, look not idly on, neither pass by on the other side, but fly to his relief. If he be deceived, tell him the *Truth;* if he be calumniated, vindicate his cause; for, although he may have erred, still recollect that indiscretion in him should never destroy humanity in you.

Finally, Sir Knight, as *memento mori* is deeply engraved on all sublunary enjoyments, let us ever be found in the habiliments of righteousness, traversing the straight path of rectitude, virtue and true holiness; so that, having discharged our duty here below, performed the pilgrimage of life, burst the bands of mortality, passed over the Jordan of death, and safely landed on the broad shore of eternity, there, in the presence of myriads of attending angels, we may be greeted as brethren, received into the arms of the BLESSED IMMANUEL, and forever made to participate in his HEAVENLY KINGDOM.

BURIAL SERVICE

OF THE

ORDERS OF MASONIC KNIGHTHOOD.

(NOTE.—The following beautiful and impressive burial service was prepared by M. E. Sir Knight, John L. Lewis, Jr., at the request of the Grand Commandery of New York.

It has been somewhat abridged in the following pages by omitting a portion of the services at the grave. If found to be still too long for any particular occasion, those portions enclosed in [ ] may be omitted; but this will seldom be found necessary in practice. The military usage of "left in front" should be observed in moving *to* the grave; but, in all cases, the order "right in front" should be followed in returning *from* the grave. This is consistent with the semi-military organization of a commandery. In moving *to* the grave, the Sir Knights should march with swords *reversed*. In returning *from* the grave, the swords should be at a *carry*.)

GENERAL REGULATIONS.

1. No Sir Knight can be buried with the funeral honors of Knighthood, unless he be a Knight Templar in regular standing.

2. It shall be the duty of the Eminent Commander to convene the Sir Knights of the Commandery, upon notice of the death of a Sir Knight who may be entitled to receive funeral honors, upon request made when living, or by his family after his decease, for the purpose of attending the funeral ceremonies.

3. Sir Knights, on such occasions, will attend in full uniform, pursuant to the regulations; their sword-hilts and the banner of the Commandery being suitably dressed in mourning.

4. On the coffin of the deceased Sir Knight will be placed his hat and sword; and if an officer, his jewel, trimmed with crape.

5. The Eminent Commander will preside during the services, and, assisted by the Prelate, lead in the ceremonies, pursuant to the Ritual. If Grand Officers or Past Grand Officers be present, they will be allotted a place in the procession according to their rank; and if the Grand Prelate, or a Past Grand Prelate, be present, he will take the place of the Prelate.

6. The Sir Knights will assemble at their Asylum, and march to the residence of the deceased, in the usual order. On arriving at the house, the Eminent Commander receives the body, placing the hat and sword, as above directed.

7. The line is then formed in column of threes, sections or platoons, *left in front*, the body, with the mourners, being in rear of the Sir Knights. The Sir Knights will be in command of the Junior Warden while marching to the grave; the officers being in the rear, according to rank: that is, the Eminent

Commander last; the Prelate being preceded by the Holy Writings, carried on a cushion, and arms and hat of the deceased borne in the rear of the Eminent Commander: if the services are to be performed by the Master Masons, then the Sir Knights should act as escort to them: in any case, the body whose duty it is to perform the last rites march immediately in front of the hearse.

8. When the public or religious services are concluded, the face of the deceased will be uncovered, and the Sir Knights (or a detachment of them) will form the "cross of steel" over the body; the Eminent Commander, with the Prelate, being at the head of the coffin, and the other officers at the foot.

9. When more convenient or desirable, the part of the service before going to the grave, as here indicated, may be performed at the house of the deceased, or be deferred till at the grave.

The funeral service of Knighthood will be conducted according to the following—

RITUAL.

EMINENT COMMANDER. Sir Knights—In the solemn rites of our Order we have often been reminded of the great truth, that we were born to die. Mortality has been brought to view, that we might more earnestly seek an immortality beyond this fleeting life, where death can come no more forever. The sad and mournful funeral knell has betokened that another spirit has winged his flight to a new state of existence. An alarm has come to the door of our Asylum, and the messenger was Death; and none presumed to say to the awful presence, "Who dares approach?" A pilgrim warrior has been summoned, and "there is no discharge in that war." A burning taper of life in our commandery has been extinguished, and none save the High and Holy One can relight it. All that remains of our beloved companion Sir Knight lies mute before us; and the light of the eye and the breathing of the lips, in their language of fraternal greeting, have ceased for us forever on this side of the grave. His sword, vowed only to be drawn in the cause of truth, justice, and rational liberty, reposes still in its scabbard, and our arms can no more shield him from wrong or oppression.

The Sir Knights here return arms.

[It is meet at such a time that we should be silent, and let the words of the Infinite and Undying speak, that we may gather consolation from his revelations, and impress upon our minds lessons of wisdom and instruction, and the meetness of preparation for the last and great change which must pass upon us all.

Let us be reverently attentive while Sir Knight our Prelate reads to us a lesson from the Holy Scriptures.

PRELATE. Help, Lord! for the faithful fail from among the children of men.

RESPONSE. Help us, O Lord!

PRELATE. The righteous cry, and the Lord heareth, and delivereth them out of all their troubles.

RESPONSE. Hear us, O Lord!

PRELATE. The Lord is nigh unto them that are of a broken heart, and saveth such as be of a contrite spirit.

RESPONSE. Be nigh unto us, O Lord!

PRELATE. The Lord redeemeth the souls of his servants; and none of them that trust in him shall be desolate.

RESPONSE. Redeem us, O Lord!

PRELATE. For I will not trust in my bow, neither shall my sword save me.

RESPONSE. Redeem us, O Lord!

PRELATE. But God will redeem my soul from the power of the grave; for he shall receive me.

RESPONSE. Redeem us, O Lord!

PRELATE. Wilt thou show wonders to the dead? shall the dead arise and praise thee? Shall thy loving kindness be declared in the grave, or thy faithfulness in destruction?

RESPONSE. Save us, O Lord!

PRELATE. We spend our years as a tale that is told. The days of our years are threescore years and ten; and if by reason of strength they be fourscore years, yet is their strength labor and sorrow; for it is soon cut off, and we fly away. So teach us to number our days, that we may apply our hearts unto wisdom.

RESPONSE. Teach us, O Lord!

PRELATE. For he knoweth our frame; he remembereth that we are dust. As for man, his days are as grass; as a flower of the field he flourisheth. For the wind passeth over it, and it is gone; and the place thereof shall know it no more. But the mercy of the Lord is from everlasting to everlasting upon them that fear him.

RESPONSE. Show mercy, O Lord!

PRELATE. We shall not all sleep, but we shall all be changed, in a moment, in the twinkling of an eye, at the last trump; for the trumpet shall sound, and the dead shall be raised incorruptible, and we shall be changed. For this corruptible must put on incorruption, and this mortal must put on immortality. So when this corruptible shall have put on incorruption, and this mortal shall have put on immortality, then shall be brought to pass the saying that is written, Death is swallowed up in victory. O death! where is thy sting? O grave! where is thy victory?

RESPONSE. O death! where is thy sting? O grave! where is thy victory?

PRELATE. The sting of death is sin, and the strength of sin is the law. But thanks be to God, which giveth us the victory through our Lord Jesus Christ.

RESPONSE. Thanks be to God.

EMINENT COMMANDER. Shall the memory of our departed brother fade from among men?

RESPONSE. It is cherished in our soul forever.

EMINENT COMMANDER. Shall no record be left of his virtues and worth?

RESPONSE. It is inscribed upon our hearts; it is written in our archives: the heart may cease to throb, and the archives may moulder and decay; but the tablets of the Recording Angel on high can never perish.

The Recorder here opens the Book of Records of the Commandery, on which a page is set apart, suitably inscribed, and says—

Here it is written.

The Sir Knights uncover, and bow their heads.

EMINENT COMMANDER. He was a true and courteous knight, and has fallen in life's struggle full knightly with his armor on, prepared for knightly deeds.

PRELATE. Rest to his ashes, and peace to his soul!

RESPONSE. Rest to his ashes, and peace to his soul!

PRELATE. Sovereign Ruler of the Universe! into thy hands we devoutly and submissively commit the departed spirit.

RESPONSE. Thy will be done, O God!]

The following Hymn will be sung:—

Precious in the sight of Heaven
  Is the scene where Christians die;
Souls with all their sins forgiven
  To the courts of glory fly.

Here above our brother weeping,
  Thro' our tears we seize this hope,
He in Jesus sweetly sleeping,
  Shall awake to glory up.

Knights of Christ! your ranks are broken!
  Close your front—the foe is nigh!
Shield to shield, behold the Token,
  As he saw it in the sky!

By this sign, so bright, so glorious,
You shall conquer! if you strive;
And like him, though dead, victorious,
In the sight of Jesus live.

The following PRAYER will then be made by the Prelate (or an extemporaneous prayer may be made by him, or by any clergyman present, as may be preferred):

FATHER OF LIGHTS! in this dark and trying hour of calamity and sorrow, we humbly lift our hearts to thee. Give us, we pray, that light which cometh down from above. Thou hast mercifully said, in thy Holy Word, that the bruised reed thou wouldst not break: remember in mercy, O Lord! before thee. [Be thou, at this hour, the father of the fatherless, and the widow's God. Administer to them the consolations which they so sorely need.] Cause us to look away from these sad scenes of frail mortality to the hopes which lie beyond the grave, and bind us yet closer together in the ties of brotherly love and affection. While we see how frail is man, and how uncertain the continuance of our lives upon the earth, and are reminded of our own mortality, lead us by thy grace and spirit to turn our thoughts to those things which make for our everlasting peace; and give us a frame of mind to make a proper improvement of all the admonitions of thy providence, and fix our thoughts more devotedly on thee, the only sure refuge in time of need. And at last, when our earthly pilgrimage shall be ended, "when the silver cord shall be loosed, and the golden bowl be broken," oh! wilt thou, in that moment of mortal extremity, be indeed *Immanuel*—Christ with us? May "the lamp of thy love" dispel the gloom of the dark valley, and we be enabled, by the commendations of thy Son, to gain admission into the blessed Asylum above, and in thy glorious presence, amidst its ineffable mysteries, enjoy a union with the spirits of the departed, perfect as is the happiness of heaven, and durable as the eternity of God! *Amen!*

RESPONSE. Amen, and Amen, and Amen!

The procession will then form, and march to the place of interment in the same order as before.

On arriving at the place, while forming in order, a suitable dirge or the following hymn may be sung:—

Softly, sadly bear him forth,
  To his dark and silent bed;
Weep not that he's lost to earth,
  Weep not that his spirit's fled.

Sadly now we rest his form,
  In the tomb to moulder still;
Hoping, in th' eternal morn,
  Christ His promise will fulfill.

One last look—one parting sigh;
  Ah, too sad for words to tell;
Yet, tho' tears now dim each eye,
  Hope we still, and sigh farewell!

On reaching the grave, the Sir Knights will form a triangle around it, the base being at the foot, the Eminent Commander and Prelate being at the head of the grave, and the friends and relatives at the foot, and the services will thus proceed:

PRELATE. Sir Knights—There is one sacred spot upon the earth where the foot-falls of our march are unheeded; our trumpets quicken no pulse, and incite no fear; the rustling of our banners, and the gleam of our swords, awaken no emotion: it is the silent city of the dead, where we now stand. Awe rests upon every heart, and the stern warrior's eyes are bedewed with feelings which never shame his manhood. It needs no siege, nor assault, nor beleaguering host, to enter its walls; we fear no sortie, and listen for no battle-shout. No Warder's challenge greets the ear, nor do we wait a while with patience for permission to enter.

Hither must we all come at last; and the stoutest heart and the manliest form that surrounds me will then be led a captive, without title or rank, in the chains of mortality and the habiliments of slavery, to the King of Terrors.

But if he has been faithful to the Captain of his salvation, a true soldier of the Cross; if he has offered suitable gifts at the shrine of his departed Lord, and bears the signet of the Lion of the tribe of Judah,—then may he claim to be of that princely house, and to be admitted to audience with the Sovereign Master of heaven and earth. Then will he be stripped of the chains of earthly captivity, and clothed in a white garment, glistening as the sun, and be seated with princes and rulers, and partake of a libation, not of death and sorrow, but of that wine which is drank forever new in the Father's kingdom above.

We cannot come here without subdued hearts and softened affections. Often as the challenge comes which takes from our side some loved associate, some cherished companion in arms, and often as the trumpet sounds its wailing notes to summon us to the death-bed and to the brink of the sepulchre, we cannot contemplate "the last of earth" unmoved Each successive death-note snaps some fibre which binds us to this lower existence, and makes us pause and reflect upon that dark and gloomy chamber where we must all terminate our pilgrimage. Well will it be for our peace then, if we can wash our hands, not only in token of sincerity, but of every guilty stain, and give honest and satisfactory answers to the questions required.

The sad and solemn scene now before us stirs up these recollections with a force and vivid power which we have hitherto unfelt. He who now slumbers in that last, long, unbroken sleep of death, was our brother. With him have we walked the pilgrimage of life, and kept watch and ward together in its vicissitudes and trials. He is now removed beyond the effect of our praise or censure. That we loved him our presence here evinces; and we remember him in scenes to which the world was not witness, and where the better feelings of humanity were exhibited without disguise. That he had faults and foibles, is but to repeat what his mortality demonstrates—that he had a human nature, not divine. Over those errors, whatever they may have been, we cast, while living, the mantle of charity: it should, with much more reason, enshroud him in death. We, who have been taught to extend the point of charity even to a foe when fallen, cannot be severe or merciless toward a loved brother.

The memory of his virtues lingers in our remembrance, and reflects its shining lustre beyond the portals of the tomb. The earthen vase, which has contained precious odors, will lose none of its fragrance though the clay be broken and shattered. So be it with our brother's memory!

The Junior Warden then removes the sword and hat from the coffin, which last will then be lowered into the grave, while the Prelate repeats as follows:

PRELATE. "I am the Resurrection and the Life: he that believeth in me, though he were dead, yet shall he live; and whosoever liveth, and believeth in me, shall never die." To the earth we commit the mortal remains of our deceased brother, as we have already commended his soul to his Creator, with humble submission to Divine Providence (*here cast some earth on the coffin*). Earth to earth (*here cast again*), ashes to ashes (*here cast more earth*), dust to dust, till the morn of the resurrection, when, like our arisen and ascended Redeemer, he will break the bands of death, and abide the judgment of the great day. Till then, friend, brother, Sir Knight, farewell!

Light be the ashes upon thee, and "may the sunshine of heaven beam bright on thy waking!"

RESPONSE.—Amen, and Amen, and Amen!

The Junior Warden then presents the sword to the Eminent Commander, who says:

EMINENT COMMANDER. Our departed brother Sir Knight was taught, while living, that his sword in his hands, as a true and courteous Knight, was endowed with three most estimable qualities—its hilt with *fortitude* undaunted, its blade with *justice* impartial, and its point with *mercy* unrestrained. To this lesson, with its deep emblematical significance, we trust he gave wise heed. He could never grasp it without being reminded of the lively significance of the attributes it inculcated. He has borne the pangs of dissolving nature: may we trust that it was with the same *fortitude* that he sustained the trials of this passing existence! To his name and memory be *justice* done, as we hope to receive the like meed ourselves; and may that *mercy*, unrestrained, which is the glorious attribute of the Son of God, interpose in his behalf to blunt the sword of Divine Justice, and admit him to the blessed companionship of saints and angels in the realms of light and life eternal!

RESPONSE. Amen, and Amen, and Amen!

PRELATE. Sir Knight companions, let us pray:

ALMIGHTY AND MOST MERCIFUL GOD! we adore thee as the Sovereign Ruler of all events, both in time and for eternity. As it hath pleased thee to take from our ranks one dear to our hearts, we beseech thee to bless and sanctify unto us this dispensation of thy providence. Inspire our hearts with wisdom from on high, that we may glorify thee in all our ways. May we have thy divine assistance, O most merciful God! to redeem our misspent time; and, in the discharge of the important duties thou hast assigned us in our moral warfare here below, may we be guided by faith and humility, courage and constancy, to perform our allotted pilgrimage acceptable in thy sight, without asking a remission of years from thee! And when our career on earth is finished, and the sepulchre appointed for all the living receives our mortal bodies, may our souls, disengaged from their cumbrous dust, flourish and bloom in eternal day, and enjoy that rest which thou hast prepared for thy good and faithful servants in thy blessed Asylum of peace beyond the vails of earth! All which we ask through the mediation of our Redeemer, King of kings, and Lord of lords. *Amen!*

RESPONSE. Amen, and Amen, and Amen!

EMINENT COMMANDER. Attention, Sir Knights!

The lines are then formed, and the Cross of Steel made over the grave, and the following HYMN is sung:—

Unveil thy bosom, faithful tomb,
  Take this new treasure to thy trust,
And give these precious relics room
  To slumber in the silent dust.

So Jesus slept; God's dying Son,
  Passed through the grave, and blest the bed;
Rest here, dear friend, till from His throne
  The morning break, and pierce the shade.

Break from thy throne, illustrious morn;
  Attend, O Earth, his sovereign word;
Restore thy trust, a glorious form;
  Let him ascend to meet his Lord.

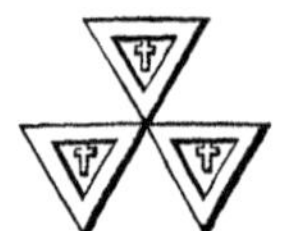

RITUAL

FOR THE USE OF THE GRAND COMMANDERY AT THE INSTALLATION OF ITS GRAND OFFICERS.

When about to proceed to the ceremony of installation, the acting Grand Commander will select some competent Sir Knight to officiate as Grand Marshal, under whose directions the officers elect will retire to the ante-room. The altar will then be placed immediately in front of the presiding officer, and the jewels of office will be placed upon it. The Grand Commander will then direct the Grand Marshal to introduce the Grand Officers elect, and display them by single line facing the East, in order of seniority, Grand Commander on the right and Grand Warder on the left; which having been accomplished, the Grand Marshal, addressing the presiding officer, will say:

RIGHT EMINENT GRAND COMMANDER: I here present before you these Eminent Sir Knights, who, having been duly elected to preside over and conduct the business of this Grand Commandery for the ensuing year, now declare themselves ready to enter upon the duties of their several stations.

The Grand Commander will then arise, call up the Grand Commandery, and address the officers elect in these words:

EMINENT SIR KNIGHTS: Before proceeding to invest you with the honors and responsibilities of your several offices, it becomes my duty to administer to you the obligation of office. Do you severally consent to take upon yourselves that obligation?

They bow in token of assent. The Grand Marshal will then cause each Sir Knight in the line of officers elect occupying the odd number from the right of the line, to draw his sword, dropping it to the left to a horizontal position. The Sir Knight on his left will lay his left hand upon the sword, then each place his right hand upon his left breast, and repeat after the Grand Commander the following

VOW OF OFFICE.

I, ———, do solemnly promise and vow, that I will maintain and support the Constitution of the Grand Encampment of Knights Templar of the United States of America, the Statutes and Regulations of the Grand Commandery of the State of Michigan, and that I will, to the best of my ability, faithfully discharge the duties of the office to which I have been elected.

The Grand Marshal will then conduct the Grand Commander elect to a position in front of the altar, and, addressing the presiding officer, will say:

RIGHT EMINENT GRAND COMMANDER: I present to you Eminent Sir —— ——, who has been elected to the office of Grand Commander, and who now declares himself ready for installation.

The presiding officer will then say:

Attention, Sir Knights—UNCOVER.

Let us unite with Sir Knight our Prelate in an invocation to the Throne of Grace.

The Prelate will pronounce the following or some other appropriate

PRAYER.

ALMIGHTY FATHER, Source of light and life, from whom cometh down every good and perfect gift; Thou who was aforetime, art now, and ever shall be, world without end. We approach Thy holy presence with deep humility, acknowledging our manifold transgressions, and supplicating a continuance of that tender mercy which has preserved us from the dangers that surround our walk through life.

Inasmuch, O Father, as Thou has promised when two or three are gathered together in Thy name, to be with them, we would beseech Thee to shed the light of Thy blessing on our present Conclave, and grant that all its purposes and all its acts may redound to Thy glory, and to the hastening of the day when all the nations of earth shall learn Thy name and bless the sacrifice of Immanuel.

Be pleased, out of Thine infinite mercy, to look upon and bless these Thy servants who are about to be invested with power to rule over and govern our Order; incline their hearts to follow after Thee; endue them with wisdom, with fortitude, with constancy and with courage to maintain the precepts of Thy holy religion, causing their good works so to shine before men that others, seeing them, may bless Thy holy name

Be with each of us here assembled; guide us in all our acts; mercifully forgive our many sins, and teach us to bear the cross, that we may finally merit the Crown of Eternal Life, thrnugh the merits of our Divine and Ascended Saviour.

Our Father, which art in heaven, hallowed be Thy name: Thy kingdom come: Thy will be done, in earth as it is in heaven. Give us this day our daily bread: and forgive us our debts as we forgive our debtors. And lead us not into temptation, but deliver us from evil: for Thine is the kingdom, and the power, and the glory forever. Amen.

The Grand Commandery will be covered, and the presiding officer will deliver the following

CHARGE TO THE GRAND COMMANDER.

RIGHT EMINENT SIR: Having been chosen by the partiality of the Sir Knights assembled in annual Conclave, to the most exalted station in their power to bestow, I offer you my sincere congratulations upon your elevation to that distinguished position, and with great pleasure invest you with the jewel of your office.

The Grand Marshal will place the jewel on the left breast of the Grand Commander.

Your long and intimate acquaintance with the rules of our Order, and with the duties of Christian Knighthood, render it unnecessary for me to recapitulate them at this time. Suffer me, however, to remind you, that the high honors of your office are accommpanied by weighty responsibilities. While, in all things pertaining to your command, your authority will at all times be respected and your orders cheerfully obeyed, yet it is expected that you will not only have a watchful care over the interests of the Order in your jurisdiction, and enforce a prompt obedience to its rules and regulations; but, that you will feel called upon to exemplify in your daily walk and conversation the excellent tenets of our profession; that your ears will never be closed to the cry of the widow and the orphan, and that you will not turn aside from injured innocence, and the wayfaring brother in distress. Maintain with unfailing care the statutes and regulations, and in your respect for law, cause all others to find the strongest incentive to obedience of all your lawful commands.

The Grand Marshal will then present the remaining Grand Officers for installation, which may be done by the Grand Commander in person, or he may waive his right in favor of the Sir Knight previously officiating. In either case the following charges will be delivered:

CHARGE TO THE DEPUTY GRAND COMMANDER.

VERY EMINENT SIR: The duties of the important station to which you have been elected are of such a nature as to require application of your utmost skill, a complete knowledge of the ritual and of the statutes and regulations governing this Grand Commandery; for you are the immediate representative of the Grand Commander, and in case of unforeseen casualty to him—which God forbid—you are to enter upon his functions and assume his responsibilities. The elevated position you are thus called to undertake demands a corresponding zeal and devotion on your part, which I doubt not, you will ever be found ready to exercise. I now invest you with the jewel of your office, and will only remind you, in conclusion, that you are henceforth on duty, and that the faithful soldier and valiant Knight sleep not at their posts.

CHARGE TO THE GRAND GENERALISSIMO.

EMINENT SIR: Having been elected to the important station of Grand Generalissimo, I take great pleasure in completing that ceremony by investing you with the appropriate jewel of your office. Your station is on the right of the Deputy Grand Commander, and the exercise of all your talents and zeal will be necessary in the discharge of your various duties. In the absence of your superior officers, the command will devolve upon you. I charge you, therefore, to be faithful to your associates; put them often in remembrance of those things which tend to their everlasting peace; be instant in season and out of season; reprove, rebuke, exhort, with all long-suffering and doctrine, ever remembering the promise, "Be thou faithful unto death, and I will give thee a crown of life."

CHARGE TO THE GRAND CAPTAIN-GENERAL.

EMINENT SIR: The office of Grand Captain-General, to which you have been elected, is one of the most important in the gift of the Grand Commandery, and I trust that in investing you with the jewel of your office, I also remind you how necessary it is that you should apply yourself with all diligence to the duties that devolve upon you.

Your station is on the left of the Grand Commander, and you are to assist him and your associate officers in council, and in their absence to govern the Grand Commandery. You are to have in charge the Grand Asylum, and see that it is in suitable array for the dispatch of business. Improve your opportunities in extending knightly courtesy and hospitality to all true and faithful Sir Knights, and in the preservation of harmony within the bounds of our jurisdiction; and whatsoever ye do, do it heartily, as unto the Lord, and not unto men; continuing fervent in prayer, watching therein with thanksgiving; ever bearing in mind the promise, "Be not weary in well doing, for in due season ye shall reap if ye faint not."

CHARGE TO THE GRAND PRELATE.

Eminent Sir: To your lot has fallen the sacred duties of the office of Grand Prelate, and in discharge of my duty I invest you with the appropriate jewel thereof. Your station will be on the right of the Grand Generlissimo, and your duty there to attend to the religious duties, as well of our Grand Conclaves as of our public ceremonials. The duties of your office are very interesting and highly important, and will require your punctual attendance at every Conclave; and may He who is able, abundantly furnish you with every good work, preserve you from falling into error—improve, strengthen, establish and perfect you, and finally greet you with, "Well done, thou good and faithful servant, enter thou into the joy of thy Lord."

CHARGE TO THE GRAND SENIOR WARDEN.

Eminent Sir: You have been elected Grand Senior Warden in this Grand Commandery, and I now invest you with the jewel of your office. Your station is at the Southwest angle of the triangle and on the right of the first division. It will be your special care to form the avenues for the approach and departure of the Grand Commander, and to prepare the lines for inspection and review. Let it be your constant care that the warrior be not deterred from duty nor the penitent molested on his journey. Finally, "Let your light so shine before men, that they, seeing your good works, may glorify our Father which is in heaven."

CHARGE TO THE GRAND JUNIOR WARDEN.

EMINENT SIR: Having been elected Grand Junior Warden, I now invest you with the jewel of your office. Your station is at the Northwest angle of the triangle, and on the left of the whole when in line, and on the right of the second and third divisions. Your duty will be to attend on all wayfaring Knights, and if found worthy, to introduce them, on the order of the Grand Commander, into the Asylum. While you are enjoined to see that they are provided with sandals, scrip and staff, you are also to keep a watch over your own actions, making them such as befit a child of humility. Truth is mighty, and those who are guided by it shall ultimately prevail; be ye therefore perfect, always abounding in the work of the Lord, that you may be a bright and shining light in the world—a city set on a hill that cannot be hid.

CHARGE TO THE GRAND TREASURER.

EMINENT SIR: You have been elected Treasurer of the Grand Commandery, and I now invest you with the official jewel of your station, which is on the right, in front of the Grand Commander. The qualities that should especially distinguish the incumbent of your station are accuracy and fidelity—accuracy, in keeping a fair and minute account of all receipts and disbursements; fidelity, in carefully preserving all the property and funds of the Grand Commandery that may lawfully come into your hands, and rendering a just account of the same whenever called upon for that purpose. Your respect for and attachment to this Grand Commandery and the great Order of which it is the organ, will doubtless stimulate you to a zealous, faithful and prompt discharge of the trust confided to you.

CHARGE TO THE GRAND RECORDER.

EMINENT SIR: By the suffrages of the Grand Commandery, you have been chosen Grand Recorder, and I now invest you with the badge of your office. In selecting a person to discharge the duties of this most important trust, the Sir Knights have unquestionably been guided by a belief that you possess in a large degree the qualities that should distinguish a Grand Recorder, which are: promptitude in issuing the notifications of his superior officers; punctuality in attending the Conclaves of the Grand Commandery; correctness in recording their proceedings; integrity in accounting for all moneys that may pass through his hands, and fidelity in paying over the same to the Grand Treasurer; and I cannot doubt your resolve to discharge these important duties with benefit to the Grand Commandery, and with honor to yourself. Your station, to which you will now repair, is on the left of the Grand Commander, in front.

CHARGE TO THE GRAND STANDARD BEARER.

EMINENT SIR: To you has been awarded the distinction of Grand Standard Bearer, and I now invest you with the jewel appropriate to that office. Your station is in the West, and in the centre of the second division. Your duty is to display, support and protect the banner of our Order, which I now place in your official custody. You will remember that, as in the olden time, it is our rallying point in time of danger, that as on the fields of Palestine, the Beauseant rarely gave back in time of battle, so now, when unfurled in the great cause of humanity, it is for you to see that it is never relinquished to an enemy, but with your life. Let, therefore, your conduct be such that the virtuous will delight to imitate it; let the refulgent rays that ever emanate from pure benevolence and humility, diffuse their lustre on all around you, that it may animate and encourage all true and courteous Sir Knights, and confound and dismay their enemies.

CHARGE TO THE GRAND SWORD BEARER.

EMINENT SIR: Having been elected Grand Sword Bearer, I now invest you with the jewel of your office. Your station is on the right of the Grand Standard Bearer, and on the right of the second division. Your duty is to watch all orders and signals from the Grand Commander, and see that they are promptly obeyed. You are also to assist in the protection of the banners of our Order, and with a heart warmly devoted to the principles of Faith, Hope and Charity; with the mystic sword that is endowed with justice and fortitude, and tempered by mercy, in your hand, you may cast your eyes upon the Standard, and remember that "*in hoc signo vinces*" is an expressive motto of our Order, and consoling to the heart of every believer.

CHARGE TO THE GRAND WARDER.

EMINENT SIR: The Grand Commandery have selected you to fill the office of Grand Warder, and I now invest you with the badge of your station. Your station is on the left of the Grand Standard Bearer, and on the left of the second division. Your duty is to observe the orders of the Grand Commander, to announce his approach and departure, as well as that of all visiting Sir Knights who may be admitted to the privileges of our Conclaves. You will therefore observe the virtue of punctuality, and by a strict observance of your important duties, merit, not only the honor now conferred upon you, but the commendation of all Sir Knights who may participate in your official courtesy.

CHARGE TO THE GRAND CAPTAIN OF THE GUARDS.

SIR ——: You have been elected to the responsible station of Grand Captain of the Guards, and I now invest you with the jewel appropriate to your office. It would be difficult to over-estimate the importance of the functions with which you are thus invested. Holding the post of danger, and therefore that of honor, your vigilance should be sleepless, your courage undaunted, and your courtesy beyond question. See to it that the avenue of approach be strictly guarded; that your courage keep all enemies at bay, while the valiant and true acknowledge in you the kind welcome due to the valiant soldiers of the cross.

The Grand Marshal will then make the following

PROCLAMATION.

In the name and by the authority of the Grand Commandery of Knights Templar of the State of Michigan, I proclaim the officers thereof duly elected and installed.

The Grand Prelate will then conclude the ceremonies by the following

CHARGE AND INVOCATION.

SIR KNIGHTS: Having now elected your officers and inducted them with appropriate ceremony into their several stations, you cannot be insensible to the duties of respect and obedience you owe them. It would indeed be a sorry compliment to your knowledge of our Order could it be supposed that you will fail in rendering them, collectively and individually, the weight of your influence in the discharge of the functions with which you have formally invested them. For, while in one sense they are but your agents, their success or failure will redound to your credit or blame, as you yourselves shall prove ready to second their lawful undertakings, and by your prompt obedience, set an example of loyalty to the constituents you represent. The past history of this Grand Commandery is a bright and open page, undimmed by any record but such as befits the gallant and true. Unquestioning fealty to the constitutions and edicts of our national organization, a warm and generous support of the office-bearers chosen to represent us before the world, and a strict adherence to the statutes and regulations of our Order, have thus far been its distinguishing characteristics ; and it now remains for you to continue the record and hand down to your successors the glorious renown acquired by your predecessors. That you will earnestly strive so to do, I cannot doubt, and I fervently pray that He who is a strong tower and defense to those who put their trust in Him may have you in His holy keeping and bless all your laudable endeavors.

Finally, my brethren, be strong in the Lord and in the power of His might. Whereof take unto you the whole armor of God, that ye may be able to withstand in the evil day, having your loins girt about with truth, and having on the breastplate of righteousness, and your feet shod with the preparation of the gospel of peace; above all, taking the shield of faith, the helmet of salvation, and the sword of the Spirit, which is the word of God.

Peace be to the brethren, and love with faith from God the Father and the Lord Jesus Christ. Amen.

Response: so mote it be.

CEREMONIES AND CHARGES

UPON CONSTITUTING AND DEDICATING A COMMANDERY, AND INSTALLING ITS OFFICERS.

The Sir Knights will assemble in the room where the ceremonies are to be performed, and open a Commandery. The jewels are then placed on the altar. An ode is then sung. The Sir Knights form a triangle around the altar and attend prayer.

The Grand Marshal will then say:

Right Eminent Grand Commander, a constitutional number of Knights Templar, duly instructed in the sublime mysteries of our Orders, and being desirous of promoting the honor of the same by aiding the cause of *Humanity*, *Knowledge*, and *Virtue*, have applied to proper authority for a warrant or charter to constitute them a regular Commandery of Knights Templar and the appendant Orders. The prayer of their petition having been granted, they are now assembled for the purpose of being legally constituted, and of having their officers duly installed in due and ancient form.

The Grand Commander will then direct the Grand Recorder to read the Charter, which being done, he will ask the members if they still approve of the officers named in the Charter; if they assent, the Grand Commander will declare:

By virtue of the high power and authority in me vested, I do now form you, my worthy brother Sir Knights, into a just and regular Commandery of Knights Templar. Henceforth you are authorized and empowered to form and open a Council of Knights of the Red Cross, a Commandery of Knights Templar and Knights of Malta, of the Order of St. John of Jerusalem, and to perform all such things as may appertain to the same; conforming in all your doings to the Laws and Constitution of the Grand Commandery under whose authority you act, and to the Constitution and Edicts of the Grand Encampment of the United States. And may the God of your fathers be with you, guide and direct you in all your undertakings.

The jewels are now uncovered to solemn music, when the Prelate rises and says:

From time immemorial, it has been customary for the Masonic fraternity to dedicate the different departments of our institution to different patrons. We dedicate our Lodges to St. John the Baptist, or the Evangelist; our Chapters to Zerubbabel, and our Commanderies to St. John the Almoner. We do this, not in that superstitious sense in which the heathen employ the term when they set apart temples for the worship of their imaginary deities, nor in that high and solemn sense in which Christians dedicate their churches to the great Jehovah; but we do it simply to testify our respect and esteem for the character of those who have been so eminently beneficial to our institution, and that their examples may stimulate us to imitate their exalted virtues.

To our most eminent and worthy patron, St. John the Almoner, I do now solemnly dedicate this Commandery, by the name and title of ——— Commandery; and may the God of all grace abundantly bless you in your laudable undertaking, and may each one of His members so redeem his time that he may receive the joyful invitation, "Enter thou into the joy of thy Lord!"

Glory to God in the highest, and on earth peace, good will towards men!

RESPONSE. As it was in the beginning, is now, and ever shall be, world without end. Amen.

INSTALLATION.

The Eminent Commander elect is then presented to the Grand Commander by the Marshal, who says:

Right Eminent, I have the honor to present to you the Eminent Sir ———, who has been elected to the office of Commander of this Commandery. I find him to be well skilled in our sublime mysteries, and observant of the noble precepts of our forefathers, and have, therefore, no doubt but he will discharge the important duties of his office with fidelity.

The Grand Commander then asks:

Eminent, are your ready to subscribe to the oath of office?

On his answering in the affirmative, the Grand Commander will draw his sword, and, holding it horizontally, the edge toward the Eminent Commander elect, who will place his left hand on the same, and his right hand on his left breast, and repeat as follows:

I, A. B., do solemnly promise, upon the honor of a Knight Templar, that I will, to the best of my knowledge and ability, faithfully discharge the various duties incumbent upon the office to which I have been elected; that I will support and maintain the By-Laws of this Commandery, and the Laws and Constitution of the Grand Commandery, under whose immediate authority I act; also, the Constitution and Edicts of the Grand Encampment of the United States of America.

The Grand Commander will then address the Eminent Commander elect as follows:

Eminent Sir, having been elected to the important and honorable station of Eminent Commander of this [new] Commandery, it is with unfeigned pleasure that I enter upon the discharge of the pleasing duty of installing you into your office. As the head of an institution founded upon the Christian religion, and the practice of the Christian virtues, you will sensibly realize the great responsibility of the new relation in which you now stand to your brethren; and, I am fully persuaded, will so conduct the important interests about to be committed to your hands, as to reflect honor upon yourself and credit upon your Commandery. It now, Sir Knight, becomes my duty to propose certain questions to you, relative to your office, to which I must request unequivocal answers:

I. Do you solemnly promise, upon the honor of a Knight Templar, that you will redouble your endeavors to correct the vices, purify the morals, and promote the happiness of those of your brethren who have attained this magnanimous Order?

II. That you will never suffer your Commandery to be opened, unless there be present nine regular Sir Knights of the Order?

III. That you will not confer the Orders upon any one who has not shown a charitable and humane disposition, or who has not made a considerable proficiency in the foregoing degrees?

IV. That you will promote the general good of our Order, and on all proper occasions be ready to give and receive instructions, and particularly from the General and State Grand Officers?

V. That, to the utmost in your power, you will preserve the solemnities of our ceremonies, and behave, in open Commandery, with the most profound respect and reverence, as an example to your brethren?

VI. That you will not acknowledge or have intercourse with any Commandery that does not work under a constitutional warrant or dispensation?

VII. That you will not admit any visitor into your Commandery who has not been knighted in a Commandery legally constituted, without his first being formally healed?

VIII. That you will pay due respect and obedience to the instructions of the General and State Grand Officers, particularly relating to the several lectures and charges, and will resign the chair to them, severally, when they may visit your Commandery?

IX. That you will support and observe the Constitution of the Grand Encampment of the United States, and the Statutes and Regulations of the Grand Commandery under whose authority you act?

X. That you will bind your successor in office to the observance of the same rules to which you have now assented?

Do you submit to all these things, and do you promise to observe and practice them faithfully?

Assents.

CHARGE TO THE EMINENT COMMANDER.

T Eminent, you will now permit me to invest you with this badge of your office. It is a Cross, surmounted by Rays of Light. It is an appropriate and beautiful emblem of the sublime principles of this magnanimous and Christian Order of Knighthood. The Cross will remind you of

Him who offered up His life as a propitiation for the sins of the world; and the refulgent rays that emanate from it, of those divine teachings and sublime precepts which He has left to guide and direct us in the paths of truth and holiness.

I present you the Charter of your Commandery. You will receive it as a sacred deposit, and never permit it to be used for any other purposes than those expressed in it, and safely transmit it to your successor in office.

I also commit to your hands the Holy Bible, the Great Light in every degree of Masonry, together with the Cross Swords. The doctrines contained in this sacred volume create in us a belief in the existence of the eternal Jehovah, the one only true and living God, the Creator and Judge of all things in heaven and earth; they also confirm in us a belief in the dispensation of His providence. This belief strengthens our Faith, and enables us to ascend the first step of the Grand Masonic Ladder. This Faith naturally produces in us a Hope of becoming partakers in the promises expressed in this inestimable gift of God to man, which Hope enables us to ascend the second step. But the third and the last being Charity, comprehends the former, and will continue to exert its influence when Faith shall be lost in sight, and Hope in complete enjoyment.

The Cross Swords, resting upon the Holy Bible, are to remind us that we should be "strong in the Lord, and in the power of His might;" that we should "put on the whole armor of God," to be able to wrestle successfully against principalities and powers, and spiritual wickedness in high places.

I also present to you the Constitution of the Grand Encampment of the United States of America; the Statutes and Regulations of the Grand Commandery of this State, and the By-laws of your Commandery. You will frequently consult them yourself, and cause them to be read for the information of your Commandery, that all, being informed of their duty, may have no reasonable excuse to offer for the neglect of it.

And now, Eminent, permit me to induct you into the chair of your Commandery, and, in behalf of the Sir Knights here assembled, to offer you my most sincere congratulations on your accession to the honorable station you now fill. It will henceforth be your special duty to preserve inviolate the Laws and Constitutions of the Order; to dispense justice, reward merit, encourage truth, and diffuse the sublime principles of universal benevolence. You will distribute alms to poor and weary pilgrims traveling from afar; feed the hungry; clothe the naked; and bind up the wounds of the afflicted. You will inculcate the duties of charity and hospitality, and govern your Commandery with justice and moderation And finally, my brother, may the bright example of the illustrious heroes of former ages, whose matchless valor has shed undying lustre over the name of Knight Templar, encourage and animate you to the faithful performance of every duty.

Sir Knights, behold your Commander.

The Sir Knights rise and present arms.

Recollect, Sir Knights, that the prosperity of your Commandery will as much depend on your support, assistance, and obedience, as on the assiduity, fidelity, and wisdom of your Commander.

The remainder of the officers are then duly qualified, by taking the oath of office, in the form and manner before stated. The Grand Marshal then presents the Generalissimo.

CHARGE TO THE GENERALISSIMO.

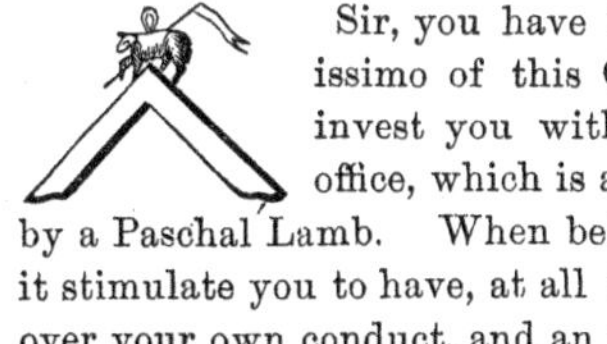

Sir, you have been elected Generalissimo of this Commandery. I now invest you with the badge of your office, which is a Square, surmounted by a Paschal Lamb. When beholding the Lamb, let it stimulate you to have, at all times, a watchful eye over your own conduct, and an earnest solicitude for the prosperity of the kingdom of the blessed Immanuel, the spotless Lamb of God, who was slain from the foundation of the world.

The Square is to remind you that the institution of Free Masonry and the Orders of Knighthood were formerly governed by the same Grand Masters, and that the same principles of brotherly love and friendship should forever govern the members of both Orders. Your station, Sir Knight, is on the right of your Commander; your duty is to receive and communicate all orders, signs, and petitions; to assist your commander in his various duties; and, in his absence, to preside in the Commandery. The exercise of all your talents and zeal will be necessary in the discharge of your various duties. I charge you, therefore, to be faithful to the Sir Knights with whom you are associated; put them often in remembrance of those things which tend to their everlasting peace. Finally, "preach to them the word; be instant in season and out of season; reprove, rebuke, exhort with all long-suffering and doctrine;" ever remembering the promise, "Be thou faithful unto death, and I will give thee the crown of life."

CHARGE TO THE CAPTAIN-GENERAL.

Sir, you are elected Captain-General of this Commandery. I now invest you with the badge of your office, which is a Level, surmounted by a Cock. As the undaunted courage and valor of the cock stimulates him to conquer his competitor, or yield himself a victim to the contest, so should you be stimulated to the discharge of every duty. You should have on "the breast-plate of righteousness," so that with patience and meekness you may ever travel on the *level* of humility, and be so supplied with divine grace as to prevent you from selling your God or denying your Master. Your station is on the left of your Commander. Your duty, among other things, is to see that the proper officers make all due preparations for the various meeting of the Commandery; that the Council Chamber and Asylum are in suitable array for the introduction of candidates and the dispatch of business. You are also to receive and communicate all orders issued by the Eminent Commander, through the officers of the line. You are to assist in Council, and, in the absence of your Commander and Generalissimo, you are to govern the Commandery. The distressed widow, the helpless orphan, and the innocent of the weaker sex, you are ever to assist and protect. But, above all, you are to stand forth, having your loins girt about with Truth, in defense of the Christian religion from all its enemies. And now, I exhort you, that with fidelity you perform every duty; and "whatsoever ye do, do heartily as to the Lord, and not unto men: continue in prayer, and watch in the same with thanksgiving;" ever bearing in mind the promise, "Be not weary in well-doing, for in due time you shall reap, if ye faint not."

CHARGE TO THE PRELATE.

Sir, you are elected Prelate of this Commandery. I have the pleasure of investing you with this Triple Triangle, which is the badge of your office, and a beautiful emblem of the Eternal Great Jehovah. Your station is on the right of the Generalissimo; your duty is to officiate at the Altar; to offer up prayers and oblations to Deity. The duties of your office are very interesting and highly important, and will require your early and punctual attendance at every meeting. Your jewel is to remind you of the importance of the trust reposed in you; and may "He who is able, abundantly furnish you for every good work, preserve you from falling into error, improve, strengthen, establish, and perfect you;" and finally greet you with, "Well done, good and faithful servant, enter thou into the joy of thy Lord."

CHARGE TO THE SENIOR WARDEN.

Sir, you are elected Senior Warden of this Commandery. I now invest you with the badge of your office, which is a Hollow Square and Sword of Justice. It is to remind you that, as the children of Israel marched in a hollow square in their journey through the wilderness, in order to guard and protect the Ark of the Covenant, so should you be vigilant in guarding every avenue from innovation and error. Let the sword of justice, therefore, be ever drawn to guard the Constitution of the Order. Your station is at the southwest angle of the triangle, and upon the right of the first division. You will attend pilgrim warriors traveling from afar, comfort and support pilgrim penitents, and recommend them, after due trial, to the favor and protection of the Eminent Commander. You will be assiduous in teaching your division their duties and exercises. You will on all occasions form the avenues for the approach and departure of your Commander, and prepare the lines for inspection and review. Let it be your constant care that the warrior be not deterred from duty, nor the penitent molested on his journey. Finally, "Let your light so shine before men, that they, seeing your good works, may glorify your Father which is in heaven."

CHARGE TO THE JUNIOR WARDEN.

Sir, you are elected Junior Warden of this Commandery. I now invest you with the badge of your office, which is an Eagle and Flaming Sword. It is to remind you to perform your various duties with justice and valor, having an eagle eye on the prosperity of the Order. Your station is at the northwest angle of the triangle, and on the left of the third division. Your duty is to attend weary pilgrims traveling from afar, conduct them on their journey, plead their cause, and, by permission of the Eminent Commander, introduce them into the Asylum. You will be careful that, in addition to the sandals, staff, and scrip, their whole preparation and deportment shall be such as to cause them to be recognized as children of humility. Teach that "*Magna est Veritas et Prævalebit,*" is the motto of our Order; and although, in the course of their pilgrimage, they will often find the heights of fortune inaccessible, and the thorny path of life crooked, adverse, and forlorn, yet, by faith and humility—courage, constancy, and perseverence in the great duties set before them in the gospel—they may gain admission into the Asylum above; there to enjoy the honor and rewards that await the valiant soldiers of the Lord Jesus Christ. Finally, be ye perfect, always abounding in the work of the Lord, that ye may be a shining light in the world. A city that is set on a hill cannot be hid.

CHARGE TO THE TREASURER.

Sir, you are elected Treasurer of this Commandery. I now invest you with the badge of your office. Your station is on the right of the Eminent Commander, in front. The qualities which should recommend a Treasurer are accuracy and fidelity—accuracy, in keeping a fair and minute account of all receipts and disbursements; fidelity, in carefully preserving all the property and funds of the Commandery that may be placed in his hands, and rendering a just account of the same whenever he is called upon for that purpose. I presume that your respect and attachment to the Commandery, and your earnest solicitude for a good name, which is better than precious ointment, will prompt you to the faithful discharge of the duties of your office.

CHARGE TO THE RECORDER.

Sir, you are elected Recorder of this Commandery. I now invest you with the badge of your office. Your station is on the left of the Eminent Commander, in front. The qualities which should recommend a Recorder are, promptitude in issuing the notifications and orders of his superior officers; punctuality in attending the meetings of the Commandery; correctness in recording their proceedings; judgment in discriminating between what is proper and what is improper to be committed to writing; integrity in accounting for all moneys that may pass through his hands, and fidelity in paying the same over into the hands of the Treasurer. The possession of these good qualities, I presume, has designated you as a suitable candidate for this important office; and I cannot entertain a doubt that you will discharge its duties beneficially to the Commandery and honorably to yourself. And when you shall have completed the record of your transactions here below, and finished the term of your probation, may you be admitted into the celestial asylum of saints and angels, and find your name recorded in the Lamb's Book of Life!

CHARGE TO THE STANDARD BEARER.

Sir, you are elected Standard Bearer of this Commandery. I now invest you with the badge of your office, which is a Plumb, surmounted by a Banner. Your station is in the West, and in the centre of the second division. Your duty is to display, support, and protect the Standard of the Order, which I now, with pleasure, confide to your valor. You will remember that it is our rallying point in time of danger; and when unfurled in a just and virtuous cause, you will never relinquish it to an enemy but with your life. Let, therefore, your conduct be such as all the virtuous will delight to imitate; let the refulgent rays which ever emanate from pure benevolence and humility, diffuse their lustre on all around, that it may encourage and animate all true and courteous Knights, and, at the same time, confound and dismay all their enemies.

CHARGE TO THE SWORD BEARER.

Sir, you are elected Sword Bearer of this Commandery. I now invest you with the badge of your office, which is a Triangle and Cross Swords. Your station is on the right of the Standard Bearer, and on the right of the second division when in line. Your duty is to watch all orders and signals from the Eminent Commander, and see that they are promptly obeyed. You are also to assist in the protection of the banners of the Order, and with a heart lively devoted to the principles of Faith, Hope and Charity; with the mystic sword that is endowed with justice and fortitude, and tempered with mercy, in your hand, you may cast your eyes upon the Standard, and remember that "*In Hoc Signo Vinces*" is an expressive motto of our Order, and consoling to the heart of every believer.

CHARGE TO THE WARDER.

Sir, you are elected Warder of this Commandery. I now invest you with the badge of your office, which is a square plate, with a Trumpet and Cross Swords engraved thereon. Your station is upon the left of the Standard Bearer, and upon the left of the second division, when formed in line. Your duty is to announce the approach and departure of the

Eminent Commander; to post the sentinels and see that the Asylum is duly guarded. You will, also, report all petitions from visitors and strangers, and communicate the orders of your superior officers; and I charge you to be punctual in your attendance at our meetings, and indefatigable in the discharge of your important duties; for though yours is among the last offices in the Commandery, it is by no means the least in importance.

CHARGE TO THE THREE GUARDS.

Sir Knights, you are appointed Captains of the Guard. I now invest you with the badge of office, which is a Square Plate with a Battle Axe engraved thereon. Your post is that of honor as well as danger. You will, therefore, be vigilant, and challenge with spirit, examine with caution, admonish with candor, relieve cheerfully, protect with fidelity, and fight valiantly.

CHARGE TO THE COMMANDERY.

Sir Knights—To manage and conduct the concerns of a Commandery of Knights Templar with that promptitude, integrity and skill which the institution demands, will require the exercise of all the talents and perseverance of its officers and members. Are any of you solicitous that your equals and inferiors should conduct themselves toward you with deference and respect? you will be sure to let no opportunity pass without furnishing them an example in your own conduct toward your superiors. The officers will recollect that those moral and religious duties and precepts which they, from time to time, so forcibly impress upon the minds of others, should by no means be neglected by themselves: and the most effectual way to insure success is to let precept and example go hand in hand.

I would therefore exhort one and all of you to look well to the East, to the West, to the North, and to the South, and see that the entering avenues are strictly guarded, and that you suffer no one to pass the threshold of your Asylum but the worthy children of humility, and, at the same time, that you suffer no one to walk among you disorderly without admonition or reproof. While such is the conduct of the officers and members, you may rest assured that this valiant, magnanimous Order will forever flourish like the green bay tree. And now, my worthy Sir Knights, I would address you in the language of David to his beloved city, "Peace be within thy walls, and prosperity within thy palaces!" For my brethren and companions' sake, I will now say, Peace be with thee!

The Grand Marshal then proclaims the [new] Commandery in the following manner viz.:

In the name of the Grand Commandery of the State of ————, I proclaim this [new] Commandery, by the name of ———— Commandery, No. —, to be legally constituted, consecrated, and the officers duly installed.

After the necessary business is finished, the Commandery is closed.

KNIGHTS TEMPLAR UNIFORM.

GRAND ENCAMPMENT OF THE U. S. REGULATIONS.

The following is the uniform for a Knight Templar, as adopted by the Grand Encampment of the United States, at New York, Sept. 3, 1862, and earnestly recommended to be adopted by all Knights Templar throughout its jurisdiction:

FULL DRESS.—Black frock coat, black pantaloons, scarf, sword, belt, shoulder-straps, gauntlets, and chapeau, with appropriate trimmings.

FATIGUE DRESS.—Same as full dress; except for chapeau a black cloth cap, navy form, with appropriate cross in front; and for gauntlets, white gloves.

SCARF.—Five inches wide in the whole, of white, bordered with black one inch on either side; a strip of navy lace, one-fourth of an inch wide, at the inner edge of the black. On the front centre of the scarf, a metal star of nine points, in allusion to the nine founders of the Temple Order, enclosing the Passion Cross, surmounted by the Latin motto, "*In Hoc Signo Vinces;*" the star to be three and three-quarters inches in diameter. The scarf to be worn from the right shoulder to the left hip, with the ends extending six inches below the point of intersection.

CHAPEAU.—The military chapeau, trimmed with black binding, one white and two black plumes, and appropriate cross on left side.

GAUNTLETS.—Of buff leather, the flap to extend four inches upward from the wrist, and to have the appropriate cross embroidered in gold, on the proper colored velvet, two inches in length.

SWORD.—Thirty-four to forty inches, inclusive of scabbard, helmet head, cross handle, and metal scabbard.

BELT.—Red enameled or patent leather, two inches wide, fastened round the body with buckle or clasp.

SHOULDER STRAPS.—*For Grand Master and Past Grand Master of the Grand Encampment.*—Royal purple silk velvet, two inches wide by four inches long (outside measurement), bordered with two rows of embroidery of gold three-eighths of an inch wide; the Cross of Salem embroidered, of gold, in the centre, lengthwise.

For all other Grand Officers of the Grand Encampment.—The same as the Grand Master, except for the Cross of Salem, the Patriarchal Cross, of gold, with the initials of the office respectively, embroidered, of silver (Old English Characters), at the foot of the cross, narrow-wise of the strap.

For the Officers and Past Grand Officers of a Grand Commandery.—Bright red silk velvet, two inches wide by four inches long, bordered with one row of embroidery of gold, quarter of an inch wide; the

Templar's Cross, of gold, with the initials of the office respectively, to be embroidered (Old English Characters), in silver, on the lower end of the strap.

For the Commander and Past Commanders of Subordinate Commandery.—Emerald-green silk velvet, an inch and a-half wide by four inches long, bordered with one row of embroidery, of gold, quarter of an inch wide; the Passion Cross, with a halo, embroidered, of silver, in the centre.

For the Generalissimo.—Same as the Commander, except for the Passion Cross, the Square, surmounted by the Paschal Lamb.

For the Captain-General.—Same as the Commander, except for the Passion Cross, the Level, surmounted with the Cock.

CAP.—Navy form; black cloth, four to five inches high, narrow leather strap fastened at the sides with small metal Templar's Cross, and with appropriate cross in front.

DISTINCTIONS.—The Sir Knights will wear white metal, wherever metal appears. Commanders and Past Commanders, Grand and Past Grand Officers, gold.

CROSSES.—Sir Knights, Commanders, and Past Commanders of subordinate Commanderies, will wear the Passion Cross; Grand and Past Grand Officers of State Commanderies, the Templar Cross; Grand and Past Grand Officers of the Grand Encampment, the

Patriarchal Cross; the Grand Master and Past Grand Masters of the Grand Encampment, the Cross of Salem, which is the Patriarchal Cross, with an additional bar in the centre.

The various crosses, as designated, to be worn on the side of the chapeau and on the scabbard of the sword. Those on the chapeau to be three inches in height; on the sword one inch.

HANGINGS FOR JEWELS.—The hangings for Grand and subordinate Commanderies may remain as at present.

GRAND STANDARD.—Is of white woolen or silk stuff, six feet in height and five feet in width, made tripartite at the bottom; fastened at the top to the cross-bar by nine rings: in the centre of the field, a blood-red Passion Cross, over which is the motto, "*In Hoc Signo Vinces;*" and under, "*Non nobis Domine! non nobis, sed Nomini tuo da Gloriam!*" The cross to be four feet high, and the upright and bar to be seven inches wide. On the top of the staff, a gilded globe or ball, four inches in diameter, surmounted by the Patriarchal Cross, twelve inches in height. The cross to be crimson, edged with gold.

BEAUSEANT.—Of woolen or silk stuff, same form and dimensions as the Grand Standard, and suspended in the same manner. The upper half of this banner is black, and the lower half white.

PRELATE'S ROBES.—A full white linen or muslin robe, open behind, reaching down to within six inches of the feet; fastened around the neck below the cravat, which should be white; and having flowing sleeves reaching to the middle of the hand. A white woolen cloak, lined with white, fastened around the neck, and extending down to the bottom of the robe; on the left front a red velvet Templar Cross, six inches in width. A blue silk stole, reaching down in front to within six inches of the bottom of the robe, and having on it three Templar Crosses of red silk. Mitre of white merino, bordered with gold, lined with green, having the Red Templar Cross extending to the edges, and surmounted by a Passion Cross three inches high. The special badge of his office is a crosier.

TEMPLAR JURISPRUDENCE.

DECISIONS MADE BY SIR WILLIAM B. HUBBARD, GRAND MASTER OF THE GRAND ENCAMPMENT OF THE UNITED STATES.

ON APPEALS.—No appeal from the decision of the Eminent Commander of a Commandery lies, in any case whatever. Right or wrong, it is final, and reversible only by himself, or by the Grand Commandery or Grand Commander, in a proper way.

An appeal lies from the Subordinate Commandery to the Grand Commandery for its decision, when in session, or to the Grand Commander during its recess.

RESIGNATION.—The Eminent Commander of a Subordinate Commandery cannot, after being installed, resign his office.

DISCIPLINE.—A Subordinate Commandery may not try charges against their Eminent Commander; they may not dispossess him for the time being of his official command, nor substitute the Generalissimo in his place. But the Grand Commander of the State Grand Commandery has cognizance and ample jurisdiction over the Eminent Commander of each Subordinate Commandery.

DEBATE.—The use of "the previous question," according to the parliamentary sense of the term, has no place in Masonry. The presiding officer, when he wishes the debate to cease, rises. Masonic usage terminates discussion.

SUMMONSES.—The powers and duties of the Eminent Commander are very extensive, and among which he has the right to *summon* the members of his Commandery at his discretion; and when summoned, it is the duty of each to obey that summons.

The excuses for not complying with a summons are few indeed, and are those that have a direct or near connection with the word *impossibility*.

1. A verbal summons from the Eminent Commander is as obligatory upon the party summoned as it would were it in writing.

2. The *seal* of the Commandery is not necessary to a written summons.

3. Every Sir Knight should promptly and strictly obey the summons of his superior, or render a satisfactory excuse.

A notice in a newspaper is not a regular summons, nor can it be made a substitute for such summons. "Due and timely notice" implies a personal notice or summons, either verbal or written.

PETITIONS.—An applicant for the Orders should apply to the nearest Commandery, and one under Dispensation occupies in this respect the same position as a chartered Commandery.

FEES.—Past experience has convinced the older Sir Knights generally, that it is impolitic to confer the Orders upon Ministers of the Gospel, in preference to others, free of charge.

CHARGES.—When a Companion has been elected to receive the Orders, and complaint has been made against him in his Lodge or Chapter for un-Masonic conduct, the Orders should not be conferred upon him unless he should be honorably acquitted. It is competent for the Commandery to stay action as to advancing a candidate at any stage of its proceedings.

Commanderies, unlike their preceding Masonic Orders, may *adjourn*.

The word "*Orders*" should always be used instead of "*Degrees*."

A non-officiated member of the Order has no right to the charity fund of the Order, or to Masonic burial rites.

BY SIR BENJAMIN B. FRENCH, GRAND MASTER OF THE GRAND ENCAMPMENT, 1862.

Honorary membership does not entitle the Sir Knight holding it to vote in a Commandery.

The Sir Knight named in a Dispensation as Commander, who never has been elected and installed a Commander, is not entitled to the rank of Past Commander.

After a clear ballot for a candidate, nothing except direct and undoubted testimony of unworthiness can interpose to prevent the conferring of the Orders.

No mere notice, without full statement of the reasons for giving it, should be regarded as of any weight. If any Sir Knight states in open Commandery that he has reasons to give why a candidate who has passed the ordeal of the ballot should not be created a Sir Knight, those reasons must be received and duly weighed.

No petition can be received signed by more than one candidate, nor can a petition be acted upon until it has been referred to a Committee and a report made.

[This decision was made in consequence of its appearing on the records of a Commandery that one petition was received from nineteen Royal Arch Masons, and, without any reference of the petition, they were all elected to receive the Order.]

Expulsion from the Order deprives a Knight Templar of all his rights as a Templar. While expelled he is driven from the Order; has no Templar standing, and although he may be restored to his standing as a Knight by a majority vote, he cannot be restored to membership in the Commandery of which he was a member when expelled, except by being regularly elected by a unanimous ballot.

The loss of a leg is an insurmountable objection to the creating a man a Knight Templar.

The present Commander of a chartered Commandery should not, at the same time, hold the office of Commander in another Commandery under Dispensation.

It is improper to dedicate a Commandery under Dispensation, or to install its officers.

It is always in the power of the Eminent Commander to order his Commandery to appear either in full costume or fatigue dress, as he may think proper.

Any Knight Templar in good standing is eligible to any office that the Grand Encampment, Grand Commandery, or a Subordinate Commandery, may think proper to bestow upon him.

The action of a Blue Lodge in suspending or expelling a Master Mason who is a Knight Templar, should affect his standing in the Commandery. No Templar can hold Masonic intercourse with an expelled Master Mason.

Any officer of a Commandery, *except the Commander*, can resign. The Commander cannot.

The following decisions were made and adopted by the Grand Encampment of the United States at its Convention, September 5th, 1865:

A Grand Commander has the power to make such assessments upon Subordinates as may be necessary for the support of the Grand Commandery.

The only test to which a candidate should be subjected is, that he is a Royal Arch Mason. It would be an improper innovation in the by-laws of any Commandery to require that a candidate should be a Royal and Select Master.

A Grand Commandery has the power to confer the

Orders of Knighthood, and to do so with or without fees, as they may deem most expedient. It is, however, a power that should be exercised with great caution, and only on extraordinary occasions.

Commanderies having exclusive power to decide all questions concerning membership, must decide all questions concerning petitions therefor by vote, such as whether or not a petition may be withdrawn, etc.

There is no remedy where a member of a Commandery persists in casting a black ball. The ballot *must* be *secret* and it *must be sacred*. It is a right that any member has, which cannot be questioned or interfered with, to reject whomsoever he pleases, and his motive cannot be questioned.

In voting for admission into the Order, every member present should be required to cast his ballot, or be excused therefrom *by a vote of the Commandery*.

The following decisions were promulgated by M. E. Sir HENRY L. PALMER, at the Triennial Conclave of the Grand Encampment of the United States, in September, 1868:

1. Any member of a Commandery, in good standing, is eligible to the office of Eminent Commander, notwithstanding he may never have held either the office of Captain-General or Generalissimo.

2. The officers of a Commandery should be elected on the day prescribed in the By-Laws of the Com-

mandery for that purpose. It is not necessary that they should be elected on Good Friday.

3. The questions having been submitted to me by letter, I determined, for the purpose of uniformity, that whenever two or more Commanderies appear in public together, the command of the whole devolves upon the Commander of the senior Commandery; and,

4. That in such case the senior Commandery is entitled to the right of the line; adding, however, that a proper exercise of knightly courtesy would, under the circumstances stated, always yield the command to the most experienced and most efficient Commander present, and the right of the line to the best drilled and best equipped Commandery.

5. No one can properly be a member of our Order, which is "founded on the Christian religion and the practice of the Christian virtues," who is not a firm believer in the religion of Jesus Christ; no one who does not acknowledge him as the Saviour of mankind, and believe in the atonement offered up by Him on Calvary, can be a worthy Knight Templar. The rules of the Order, however, do not require any further or more definite profession of faith than is comprehended in the ritual. One who ridicules or makes light of the Holy Bible, or scoffs at religion, is an unworthy member of the Order.

6. A Knight Templar in good standing has the right to object to conferring the Orders of Knighthood

upon a Companion Royal Arch Mason in his Commandery, after such Companion has been balloted for and declared elected; and this, whether the objecting Sir Knight was present at the time of balloting or not; and when such objection is made in open Commandery, verbally or by a formal communication thereto in writing, the Eminent Commander is not authorized to proceed and confer the Orders upon the candidate. The Sir Knight making the objection cannot be required to disclose his reasons therefor.

7. Every member of a Commandery, in good standing, has a right to know what transpires in his Commandery, but no member of a Commandery should disclose to any one not a member any matters arising during the hours of a regular assembly; nor should any Sir Knight disclose anything transpiring in a Commandery to an absent member, which might be productive of discord and unkind feeling. It should be the constant care of all Knights Templar to promote harmony and concord, not only in their own Commanderies, but among all the members of the Order within the circle of their acquaintance.

8. An Eminent Commander cannot resign his office during the term for which he is elected, after being duly installed.

9. To the question, "Can a Sir Knight be an active member and enjoy all the privileges and rights of two Commanderies at the same time, one of them being under Dispensation?" I answered: He cannot. When a Templar signs a petition for a Dispensation

to form a new Commandery, if the Dispensation be granted, his membership in his old Commandery remains in abeyance, and he is an active member of the new Commandery while under Dispensation; and if the Dispensation be followed by a charter to the new Commandery, he continues to be a member of that and ceases to be a member of the old one.

10. That whenever a Grand Commander removes from the jurisdiction of his Grand Commandery, he thereby vacates his office, the powers of which devolve upon the Deputy and remainlng officers, according to seniority. That as a permanent removal from the jurisdiction vacates the office of the Grand Commander, it follows, as a necessary consequence, that after such removal he cannot exercise the powers of the office.

11. That a Commandery under Dispensation has the same exclusive jurisdiction within the territory which, in case a charter should be obtained, would belong to it, that would appertain to a chartered Commandery.

12. That in the absence of any provision in the By-Laws of a Commandery to the contrary, the petition of a Companion who is rejected may be presented at any regular meeting subsequent to that at which the rejection occurs.

13. The rituals of the Orders of Knighthood should not be written.

14. Upon application for the Orders of Knighthood, the vote must be by ballot. The ballot is secret,

and has the same effect as a ballot in a Lodge of Master Masons.

15. Petitions for the Orders of Knighthood can only be received and acted upon at *regular* Conclaves of the Commandery.

16. To the question, "Can a Past Commander, who is an honorary member of a Commandery, open the same, in the absence of the three principal Officers (*i. e.*, Eminent Commander, Generalissimo, and Captain-General), he being, at the time, an active member and also an officer of another Commandery?" I answered as follows: He cannot. The last clause of section four of article three of the Grand Constitution relates to Past Eminent Commanders who are members of the Commandery. Honorary membership does confer the right to vote in any Commandery, nor any rank or standing therein, but is merely complimentary.

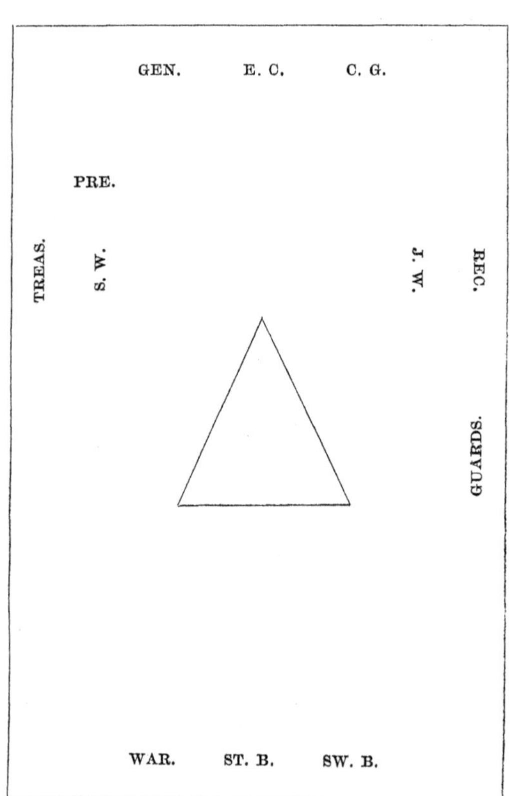

OFFICERS' STATIONS.

CONTENTS.

www.ingramcontent.com/pod-product-compliance
Lightning Source LLC
LaVergne TN
LVHW011222110826
845150LV00006B/1506

* 9 7 8 1 4 2 5 5 1 5 3 9 3 *